WHO'S BUILDING THE ARK?

HOW TO MANAGE THROUGH HELL AND HIGH WATER

CHRISTINE JAX, PH.D.

Who's Building the Ark:
How to Manage Through Hell and High Water

ISBN: 978-0-9825706-2-3 (ebook)
ISBN: 978-0-9825706-3-0 (paperback)

All characters are fictitious. Any references to people, names, characters, and places are products of the author's imagination.

Cover design by Rocko Spigolon
Interior typesetting by Vanessa Mendozzi

First printing 2020

La Finca Palabra, publisher
221 NW Fourth Avenue
Delray Beach, FL 33444

DEDICATION

Thank you to my wonderful husband and lay-editor
Jesus Castillo.

Without a doubt, we learn many of our leadership
skills from our families. My parents, Don and Mickey
Jax, made sure I had the confidence and experiences
to take my place in the world, and I hope I have done
the same for my children and my children's children.

CONTENTS

INTRODUCTION

This book is for anyone who manages people, and it will be most helpful if you have multiple levels in your vertical or if you lead an entire organization. The more complex and matrixed your organization, the more you will come to appreciate knowing who people are at their core and how this influences their thinking and behavior.

Managing people just might be the hardest thing you do. There are many personality types to juggle in any organization, and the countless personality inventories that exist provide little guidance on how to motivate and lead your cast of characters. Although these existing inventories help you assess the inner and outer workings of your employees, and probably hope you will either change how you manage, or at least understand people better, they don't provide context-specific examples and practical advice. This book will do exactly that.

As a manager, you deal with several types of resources: human, financial, physical, intellectual, and informational. The resources that are going to take the greatest amount of time, give you the most headaches, and drive the success or failure of every other resource are your human resources. Simply put, your employees will make or break you. It is important that you understand their performance metrics, but it is *essential* that you understand how they think, what motivates them, where they are best deployed, and how you can get the most out of them. This is particularly true if there is not a straight line from employees to a key revenue metric.

You have probably heard the expression "anyone can predict rain; who's building the ark." What can you really learn from this cliché that will make you a more effective leader and manager? What does it mean to predict rain in your business? Is it identifying unintended consequences, sales cycles, or risks? Something else? What about building an ark. What does that mean for you? Is it building financial reserves, managing expectations, creating competitive resiliency, ensuring risk mitigation? Or something else? Once you dig deeper into your situation and needs, you can easily use this book to understand how your employees, with their different personality types, view themselves, their positions, and others, and how you can effectively manage them.

I've used my psychology and administration degrees, as well as my decades of experience as a manager leading million- and billion-dollar organizations, to develop clearly identifiable and understandable personality types with details on traits, motivations, strengths, and challenges. With knowledge of these personality types, you can ensure you have the right people in the right places, building and maintaining your ark. Your ark is your business and it must be kept afloat and going the right direction at the right speed. Getting to know the different personality types will make a difference in how you manage people, and this will make all of the difference in your performance and the success of your organization.

THE TWENTY PERSONALITY TYPES[1]

These personality types in this book evolved from the intersection of psychology, cultural anthropology, and business management. I spent years reviewing research literature and conducting observations in order to develop, revise, and test my theories and the resulting personality types. Then I drew upon ancient and mythological archetypes to explain the personality types and ensure they could be presented in a manner that provided the clearest delineation of characteristics that would resonate with people. Additionally, because so many organizations utilize well-known personality inventories, I triangulated my findings with those instruments to ensure I did not have any concerning outliers. Placing

---

1 I have chosen to make an intentional grammatical error in the writing of the book and use the words "they," "them," and "their" where "he," "she," "him," and "her" would be more accurately used, so as not to perpetuate or develop any gender stereotypes.

the personality types into four categories resulted from a desire to provide a management tool that was intuitive and easy to use.

There are twenty personality types within four main categories. The four categories are Allies, Associates, Accomplices, and Adversaries. Knowing what category someone is in can help you quickly determine how best to deploy them in your organization. The categories are shortcuts to quickly understanding how various personality types see the world and relate to it via their employment. The twenty personality types, five within each of the four categories, break down for you how individuals see themselves so you can use that information to best manage and motivate them. The names of the personality types make it easy for you to remember and capture the essence of their demeanor and conduct.

The Allies are made up of Captains, Handlers, Advisors, Encouragers, and Enablers. The Allies are just that, people you can count on. They are reliable, good people who support you and your organization.

The Associates are the Innovators, Planners, Executors, Investigators, and Defenders. The Associates are people you can persuade to follow your lead because they want to do the right thing, but they just are not yet connected to your mission or engaged with you.

The Accomplices are the Disruptors, Preachers, Fabricators,

Schemers, and Users. The Accomplices can be deployed effectively if you can get them to believe in you and/or what you are doing, but they are not always ethical, and their loyalty is fluid.

The Adversaries are the Dictators, Blamers, Posers, Agitators, and Saboteurs. Adversaries are problematic and you need to get rid of them or manage them carefully if you have a compelling reason for keeping them.

Each personality type is going to react differently when it comes to building the ark and helping you get through hell and high water. Below are the various types of personalities in light of how they might react to God proclaiming a flood, because every manager knows…when it rains, it pours.

"A GREAT RAIN AND FLOODS
ARE COMING."

ALLIES

THE CAPTAIN	"Flooding is inevitable, so I had a blueprint for an ark designed, created a five-year strategy, and contracted with vendors for provisions."
THE HANDLER	"It's going to rain, and a flood will follow. I've purchased materials and pulled together a team to build an ark."
THE ADVISOR	"It's going to rain, but we will all be fine."
THE ENCOURAGER	"It's going to rain, but it will stop before there's a flood. And even if it floods, we'll have an ark built first."
THE ENABLER	"There will be a flood; do you want me to help build an ark or teach others to build the ark?"

ASSOCIATES

THE INNOVATOR	"It's going to rain, and a flood is inevitable. Let's build a double-decker sailboat with solar panels."
THE PLANNER	"It's going to rain, and I have a policy and process to build an ark, and we can sell it to a cruise line when the floods recede."
THE EXECUTOR	"There will be a flood, and I will ensure an ark is built. I already have bids out to the best shipbuilders."
THE INVESTIGATOR	"There will be a flood, and I've built myself a little boat to weather the storm."
THE DEFENDER	"It always rains and never floods. If it does, we can go to higher ground and wait for rescue."

ACCOMPLICES

THE DISRUPTOR	"Floods are coming, and I built a self-contained living space fueled by water."
THE PREACHER	"There might be a flood, but we can build an ark with prayer and divine guidance."
THE FABRICATOR	"I have blueprints for an ark, but I can't tell you where I got them."
THE DEVISER	"There will be a flood. I have connections, and I can save you... for the right price."
THE USER	"There will be a flood, and someone needs to figure something out."

ADVERSARIES

THE BLAMER	"It's going to flood and no one has bothered to build an ark."
THE DICTATOR	"I told you it was going to rain. Don't listen to anyone else from now on. I alone will save us when the flood comes."
THE POSER	"It's going to rain; I'll be in my office working. You all should build the ark I invented."
THE AGITATOR	"There will be a flood, and we're all going to die."
THE SABOTEUR	"It's going to flood. I wonder how the dam broke."

As a leader and manager, perhaps a Captain yourself, you have responsibility for ensuring the proper building and steering of the ark (your business), and you need the right crew at the right posts. In the following chapters, you will read detailed profiles of each personality type. You will learn how to recognize, deploy, and manage each type for optimal performance during the floods your organization will face. There are people who won't be much help during the floods, and you need to recognize them as well. Keep in mind that there are no totally bad or totally good people--although some skew hard in one direction or the other. However, some people have traits you do not need or want, and there are others who could even do harm to your organization without proper coaching, guidance, or exiting.

The first chapter of the book provides you with the overall blueprint for building your ark, the next several chapters present and explain each of the personality types, and the last chapter equips you with strategies for building and managing your ark by understanding who works best with whom, in what combinations, and how you can create the ideal climate for topnotch performance and corresponding success.

BLUEPRINT FOR BUILDING THE BEST ARK

To be a strong captain, and in order to run a tight ship, you want to put employees in the optimal job positions and provide them with opportunities for success. This is even more the case if you are facing challenges, such as downsizing, brand confusion, a lawsuit, or intense product competition. Putting your people in the best positions requires an understanding of their temperaments, characteristics, motivations, sources of fear and pleasure, and their views of others. The profiles in this book can help you quickly identify the members of your crew and put them in the positions within your organization where they are best suited to support your strategic and tactical needs. Once you get your people in the right positions, you can continue to use their profiles to guide your personnel management—but first you need to create the best hull, or framework for employee success. To accomplish this, you need to

- Engage

- Gain loyalty and trust

- Motivate to act

- Rally around goals

- Pilot performance against metrics

- Nurture skills

- Manage expectations

- Quash concerns

ENGAGING THE CREW

Employees are engaged when they understand their roles and are eager to tackle their duties. According to Gallup, 66% of the U.S. workforce is not engaged, meaning they "are not cognitively and emotionally connected to their work and workplace" (Harter, 2018). This is costing employers hundreds of billions of dollars per year in lost productivity. How much is it costing you?

In order to fully engage your employees, there are certain things you need to do. For starters, and quite simply, allow employees to be themselves. Create the conditions that will let your people feel safe enough to be themselves, and use their natural skills and abilities. One of these conditions is offering the latitude for people to ask questions and make reasonable mistakes without negative consequences. Allowing people to be themselves will limit, if not eliminate, tension at the workplace, because you can authentically get to know your employees, and they won't feel unnecessarily confined or limited.

Another key to creating engagement is finding opportunities for your employees to spend time with projects and duties that excite them. Of course, this entails giving them some flexibility to discover how they can best contribute, but it is time well spent. Similarly, find opportunities for them to be influencers on the topics they have the most exposure to or some expertise in. People can be influencers by writing blurbs for your newsletter, sharing a news clip or research at a meeting, introducing a project at a company function, or being asked, "Please share that knowledge with your colleagues whenever you have a chance."

GAINING LOYALTY AND TRUST

Employees are loyal to people, not to a company. The old adage about teachers and their students applies equally to bosses and their employees: "They won't care what you know, unless they know that you care." If you want your employees to be loyal to you and your organization, show them that they matter to you and your management team.

There are many ways to ensure employees know you care. Start by making sure all employees know the organization's mission, and more importantly, *why* it is the mission and what objectives are in place for support. Help them understand why the mission is important to you and how everyone can play a contributing part. Being loyal to you starts with employees understanding what it is you are loyal to—presumably the company's mission.

Loyalty is built on trust, so develop a culture of empowerment instead of micromanagement. Give employees stretch projects to help them build their confidence, and make sure you are not undermining it with words you think are "coaching" but are in fact demoralizing. Avoid words and phrases that shame, and never get into the rumor mill. The minute you say to a member of your team, "I heard something bad about you," or, "There is a perception about you that…" you have lost the ability to gain their loyalty. Your belief in them is what feeds their loyalty to you. Believe in your people and build them up.

Cultivate a culture of kindness. Caring for people goes beyond saying, "Good morning!" and walking around the building once in a while to see what people are up to. As a matter of fact, doing so without a genuine spirit of warmth and connectedness simply looks as if you are "checking up" on your people because you don't trust them. Kindness means knowing what is happening in people's lives. If your company is too large for you to do that yourself, make sure you know what is happening in the lives of your direct reports and get the message out that you expect them to do the same. That means knowing about special events such as birthdays, work anniversaries, marriage anniversaries, home purchases, adoptions, and births. Kindness means acknowledging significant milestones.

MOTIVATING ACTION

By nature, people seek to understand their purpose in life. "Why am I here?" and "What am I meant to do?" are life's basic questions. Find methods to help people answer those questions, and then connect the organization's mission to the employee's purpose in life. Employees can be guided to answer those questions in initial hiring interviews, in annual reviews, and in informal conversations with their direct supervisors. Asking someone what their life purpose is or how they want to make a difference may seem awkward or odd, but it won't seem that way in an environment where you are actively seeking to engage your employees. It will seem as one more indication that they are people to you first and workers second.

Providing stretch goals and stretch projects will also engender loyalty and foster motivation. Just like you, employees like to see what they are capable of, but they want to feel safe and supported when pushing themselves and their abilities. Make sure your managers all understand that stretching employees invigorates them around organizational goals, and everyone benefits from that. This is a form of both succession planning and ensuring your ark is sea-worthy for the long term.

Cross training is similar to stretch projects in that it enables employees, particularly those with promotion potential, to feel both appreciated and believed in. Cross training ensures you have the foundation you need for your organization, and if it helps an employee improve his or her resume to seek a better position elsewhere, know that you have gained an advocate for your company. Cross training rewards you by having someone to step in when an employee is out sick or vacates a position.

RALLYING THE CREW

Rallying the crew is a step above engagement. It's a way to inspire your employees to go above and beyond and to become zealous supporters of you and your organization. Think of engagement as an individual approach and rallying the crew as a group approach for when you are trying to reach significant numbers of your employees at one time. There are several ways to rally employees, such as holding launch and reveal events for new products or recognition events to honor longevity, accomplishments, or personal milestones.

Another great way to rally your employees is to create an actual rallying cry, even if it never becomes a public tagline. You can even have a competition to come up with one. Rallying cries sound like this: "XYZ, making lives better," "XYZ: leaving earth better than we found it," "The best people make the best company."

In order to rally your crew, you must first intentionally develop a positive culture that they can see and feel. Your goal is to get them to rally around this culture as much as around you and the mission of the organization. In order to get employees to rally around a culture, they have to see how the values are tied-in. These values need to be explicit and part of the lived experiences managers are intentional about creating.

PILOTING PERFORMANCE

You have to monitor performance in order to know who needs more support, coaching, a different seat on the boat, or to be let go. Piloting performance is what you do to ensure you have some control over how employees are doing. Likely, it's what you are already good at—or you would not be in a leadership position. Sometimes, however, leaders focus on strategy and tactics at the expense of directly leading their staff. You need to steer employees in the right direction as well as monitor how they are doing. You want to keep their eyes on the prize and communicate expectations as well as assessment. As a result, you should see your staff move in the direction you desire and be actively intervening with your managers when that is not happening. There should never be a surprise during a performance review. Employees should already know if they are excelling, falling short, or landing somewhere in between. Your employees should get most of this information from their direct supervisors, but as a leader, you should strive to have face time with as many people as you can. In a small company, you can have one-on-one conversations with as many people as possible. In a larger company, you should conduct such in-person conversations with mid-level managers, and in extremely large organizations, you should be having town hall meetings with question and answer sessions. Such transparency empowers you to truly pilot performance.

It is enormously beneficial to have an open-door policy whereby employees with concerns can come to you directly. Practically speaking, if you run a large organization, an open-door policy is difficult. There are two ways to get around this. The first way is to make sure your upper and middle managers understand you would like them to have an open-door policy, and the second way is for you to have an annual open-door week whereby interested employees can book an appointment with you for 15-20 minutes to share with you key concerns or ideas.

It's not enough to see and hear your employees. To ensure the success of your organization, empower workers by letting them have input into the strategies and metrics on which they are measured and held accountable. This ensures understanding, buy-in, and accountability. Praise success and coach failure. Punishing or ridiculing failure decreases an employee's willingness to take risks, and taking risks is what will uncover opportunities, release synergies, and spark innovation. Make sure those you manage understand this, particularly managers who report to you.

NURTURING SKILLS

Many employees feel rewarded with public recognition or tangible rewards, so find ways to celebrate accomplishments such as the completion of training or projects. Employee of the Month recognition (or year, for smaller companies), can bolster morale, as can specialized awards, such as "Best Team Player," "Most Inspiring Co-worker," and so on. At some organizations, when employees are thankful for the assistance or spirit of another employee, they have the opportunity to send a thank-you note, cookie, or shout-out in the company newsletter. Many companies provide sizable bonuses for upper managers who meet goals. Those managers did not meet those goals alone, so consider smaller bonuses for all employees. Gift cards between $100--$500 can go a long way in thanking employees for helping the company reach goals and milestones.

It's always a great idea to reward those who save the organization money. Encourage a climate of continuous improvement by rewarding employees with a percentage of the money they save the company or with a flat "great idea" bonus.

There is yet another perspective. Influential author Daniel H. Pink pointed out, in his book *Drive*, that focusing the attention of employees on rewards can divert their attention from actual work activities. Instead, help employees become better at what they do and give them sufficient autonomy to do it. Formalizing mentoring relationships will increase engagement as well as skill development, and who knows what will come of the increased collaboration.

Reward people with opportunities to learn and attempt new tasks, harkening back to stretch projects and cross-training. Include training opportunities in your array of skill development options. Bring in speakers and trainers, provide seminars and workshops, purchase keys to online training programs, consider unlimited book purchases as an employee benefit, and provide financial support for advanced college credit and degrees.

BUILDING CONFIDENCE

Effective leaders make sure to manage expectations because it keeps people from being disappointed, which in turn bolsters confidence because the path is clear with few or no roadblocks. Confidence feeds on itself, because employees perform better when they are confident, which creates more confidence. It's the internal production loop that ensures organizational success.

According to leadership expert and Harvard Business School professor Rosabeth Moss Kanter, author of *Confidence: How Winning Streaks and Losing Streaks Begin and End*, there are three cornerstones of confidence: accountability, collaboration, and initiative. Building confidence in your employees starts with understanding that every individual is seeking to satisfy personal needs and advance personal causes. If an employee is an ardent champion of your mission, it is because they find it personally fulfilling in some way.

Build employee confidence by understanding individual employee needs and linking accountability from that grounding to your business goals. You can do this by giving employees small goals that are both aligned to the company strategic plan as well as to what that individual employee values, as ascertained by their direct supervisor through personal conversations. This is a way to scaffold accountability. Helping people enjoy small successes bolsters their confidence to keep going toward the more daunting goals.

Integrating collaboration into the fabric of the organization through meetings, task forces, open spaces, and jointly owned goals helps employees see their importance to a team and reduces feelings of isolation. If you already have scaffolded accountability, you have employees with a foundation from which to develop collaboration. Connection with others builds confidence by giving clarity to the part each person plays in the organizational mission and strategic goals. Employees are able to personally see the small picture, the big picture, the people they can consider their teammates, and where they fit in. Collaboration helps an employee see more pieces of the puzzle and gives more relevance to their role. This gives them the courage to take initiative, whether it is to expand goals, improve processes, or increase personal performance.

QUASHING CONCERNS

Most employees are going to be fairly removed from the realities of the financial bottom line and will have to rely on rumor and/or piece together their own observations to assess how the company is doing or whether there are any problems. This is not the best way of getting to the facts. Additionally, employees will be taking this limited knowledge and filtering it through their own insecurities and fears. Some people may worry about job security, upward mobility, or even the company's reputation and viability.

The best way to quash concerns and control perceptions is to actively communicate with your employees and ensure your senior managers are modeling behavior that makes employees proud. Nothing can dissolve employee morale and confidence more quickly than senior managers who have a casual acquaintance with professional and ethical behavior. Whether you have a strong media presence or not, your employees are going to get their ethical and branding cues from your senior management team, and to a lesser degree, your social media team. The behavior of your senior management team must align with your values and ethics as well as the company mission, vision, value propositions, and brand identity. When employees are confident in leadership, they will align their thoughts and behaviors to defend those perceptions and even use those perceptions to defend against naysayers.

"A GREAT RAIN AND FLOODS
ARE COMING."

ALLIES

THE CAPTAIN

"Flooding is inevitable, so I had a blueprint for an ark designed, created a five-year strategy, and contracted with vendors for provisions."

PROFILE

The Captain is an Ally and natural leader. The Captain is what every organization needs, what boards seek, and what CEOs believe they are. Unfortunately, a title does not make one a Captain; grit, hard-work, emotional intelligence, and creativity are what do. Captains stay focused regardless of the environment, moods around them, and obstacles before them. While they have the emotional intelligence to see discontent or misalignment, they do not take on the negativity of others and let it influence them or weigh them down. They don't have time to be thin-skinned and take things personally. True Captains are not obsessed with their power but with their mission and purpose.

People do not just follow a Captain because they have the ability to dispense positions, power, and resources; they follow because they can't help it. There is ease and understanding around a Captain that causes others to want to be in their light or share in their creations. The personality of the Captain is confident and strong-willed, but others are inspired primarily because the Captain's personality is so well integrated. Others fall in line as part of a seeming natural order.

True Captains will demand attention, but it is not for ego fulfill-ment. It is to drive action. They love challenges and are relentless in their pursuit to solve problems. They believe that their knowledge and skill set mean they need to be heard and understood so essential goals can be accomplished. They also know that someone needs to be in charge. They eagerly fill that space. The Captain is a sharp observer of self, employees, the market, and social trends. The ability to quickly observe, assess, synthesize, and react gives the Captain insight, vision, and in turn the credibility that gives others the comfort to follow. This then fuels the energy others want to be part of.

Because Captains are cooperative and open, they develop real followers, as opposed to situational followers. Real followers are steadfast, and their following is not dependent upon a particular issue or event. They are fans who are not called upon to be understanding or forgiving, but instead they rise up instinctively to praise or defend. Situational followers, in comparison, only get behind a leader when a situation, event, cause, or self-interest compels them to do so. Situational followers can turn away just as quickly. Captains are transparent with their plans but careful and caring in how they disseminate information. As a result, Captains can ask their followers to give them the benefit of the doubt or ignore occasional transgressions.

Things seem to come naturally to the Captain because they are able to follow intuition or an earlier blueprint developed through previous successes. They quickly chart a course of action and therefore successfully avoid appearing idle or adrift. Whether innate or learned, Captains shows competency in their ability to assess a situation, analyze where leadership is needed and why, determine who will naturally follow and who will not, consider unintended consequences, and quickly craft a message. These abilities show-up rather early in the career of a Captain—some would argue as early as adolescence. They have street smarts, as some would say, and when a Captain seeks advanced education or a credential, it likely will be to build knowledge, develop particular skills, or refine their natural logic. They are naturally optimistic and self-assured, and this manifests itself in conscientiousness and reliability.

Captains have foresight. Because they know their company intimately, study the industry faithfully, and have an abundance of emotional intelligence, they are able to quite accurately predict what's ahead. This is a gift that keeps on giving. It helped get them where they are and keeps them there by supporting their innovative approach. They have the ability to forge ahead because they have already accounted in some detail for what everyone else just refers to hazily as "unintended consequences."

Captains can be fearless, courageous, or both. It is said that courage is not the absence of fear, but rather the conquering of it. Many Captains embody this when they conquer fear by seemingly ignoring risks and plowing through obstructions. They usually conquer fear by compartmentalizing and reprioritizing as they are in the middle of solving problems. Regardless of whether the Captain is genuinely courageous or bordering on psychopathic fearlessness, they know to rely on their instincts, experiences, and followers. Others admire their ability to jump from the proverbial frying pan into the fire, where they deftly employ analytical skills, emotional intelligence, and team insight to keep the ark from burning down.

TECHNIQUES TO MOTIVATE

The Captain loves opportunities and sees them everywhere. They are naturally engaged, unless they are in the wrong position or with the wrong company. In which case, they quickly will figure this out and correct the situation by moving on, if not moving up. Engaging the Captain means ensuring you are fully utilizing their attributes and experiences. If you are a board member working with a CEO or a CEO trying to capture the talents of a Captain below you, be sure you are treating them as a peer with whom you can also learn and grow. Utilizing the Captain fully so they are making a difference to your bottom line is what will provide them with the motivation to stay and succeed. While Captains are highly-focused, results-driven, and motivated by personal achievements, they are also highly motivated by group achievements and should never be isolated, even for short periods of time. They are meant to lead.

The Captain is relentless in pursuing results and their take charge attitude can be domineering, but true Captains also are compassionate. They can, and often do, provide safety and security to their followers. They utilize people because of their skills, but they do not use those skills simply to advance an agenda. They innately understand that utilizing people in the workplace for who they are and what they offer helps them see that they matter. This is leading as opposed to using, or worse yet, coercing. When coercion happens in an organization, it does not originate in the Captain. You will, however, see this trait demonstrated later in the book by other personalities. To get the most out of a Captain, you have to make sure they have the opportunity to build and nurture a base of people.

Captains control through structure, strong work ethic, and tight schedules. They enjoy pushing themselves and want to prove they can actually turn the ship. Captains who are not the CEO need to be given opportunities to take charge of projects that truly make a difference. This means benefitting the overall organizational agenda as well as the Captain's need to matter to the larger mission by meeting targets that make money, set a standard, or create a trend. Captains are effective and efficient drivers. You simply give the charge and get out of the way. This freedom, and your trust in them, allows them to build upon their self-motivation and solid vision.

Help the Captain use critique as a way to improve themselves and the organization and, given their strength of character, be ready to do this by playing the devil's advocate and by detailing or even modeling alternatives. Captains are driven by the head, not the heart, so be logical and practical. Captains are typically well-read, so always consider throwing an insightful book at them.

PLACE ON YOUR TEAM

The Captain is your ideal chief executive officer or president. Keep in mind however, that Captains are not always like cream, and may not automatically rise to the top. Their rise can be halted or hampered if there is not a path to the top, and at times there is not. That is why Captains generally, but not always, jump from one top level position to the next. Sometimes Captains have to take positions below their potential due to earliness in a career, a geographical move, getting laid-off, signing a non-compete clause, or a personal desire to change industries. Because of this, you may have Captains in your midst, but not on your leadership team. You can recognize them based on the above descriptions, but also based on whether they already are developing a following and have a charisma to which others seem to gravitate. If you have a leadership position open, or can create one, do so before you lose this asset. If you cannot make a move now, you can nurture the misplaced Captain in your organization by providing leadership opportunities and making sure the Captain is engaged, productive, and actively appreciated. However, the Captain will not last long in positions without power, influence, and intellectual peers.

The Captain, while ambitious, is duty-bound and mission-driven, so let the Captain represent you at conferences or with external organizations. The Captain thrives where they can take initiative, so bring the Captain in early to guide specific projects; spend time seeking advice from the Captain; show the Captain a path to something bigger, whether inside your organization or not, and ensure you have not blocked the Captain's success by having them report to an insecure supervisor who will no doubt find a way to remove this threatening persona from the organization. If you have a small organization, your Captain will be seen as a tribal chief or crone. They almost always will seem older than their years.

EXAMPLES OF CAPTAINS

John McCain

Navy Lieutenant Commander; U.S. Senator; presidential candidate

Barack Obama

Attorney; State senator; U.S. Senator; President, United States of America; Nobel Laureate

Meg Whitman

CEO, Ebay; CEO, Hewlett-Packard; California gubernatorial candidate; philanthropist

THE HANDLER

"It's going to rain, and a flood will follow. I've purchased
materials and pulled together a team to build an ark."

PROFILE

The Handler is an Ally and a key to your organization and its
success. What is "right" and socially acceptable matters deeply
to them, as does the active participation of other employees.
Because of this, and their reliance on the rule of law and dictates of
authority, they seek to build a righteous culture. First and foremost,
they seek to set a foundation on which to build an effective organization. They develop plans and processes, and they compel others
to do the same, often through their resolute yet affable ways. While
they are fiercely loyal to both the organizational leader and the
mission, they still will tend to build a foundation that works best for
themselves. They justify this because they are certain that what is
best for them is best for the organization. They have a strong sense
of self and durable confidence that has taught them that they can

take care of others once they have taken care of themselves. The Handler's ruling metaphor is the airplane safety measure that instructs put on your own oxygen mask before helping someone else.

Reliable communication and efficient problem-solving are cornerstones to Handlers, so they value the use of strong messaging systems and procedures to both support and protect their organization. Handlers are highly principled and have based their opinions on fact, so they are confident in the direction they take and the clear advice they dole out. They will do what they can to ensure the organization follows suit. The combination of reliable communication channels and trustworthy information in the control of the Handler, along with the processes they set-up, will ensure your organizational messaging is understood and respected.

Handlers are often your fixers. They are keenly aware that they keep the organization moving through their dedication to completion, and they will do whatever they need to ensure they are likewise supported. Handlers are adept communicators and listeners, or they would never be able to simultaneously please those above them as well as those below them. They are expert synthesizers who take in information like sponges, integrate it with their own knowledge, and determine the right way to communicate back to a particular audience in a way that maintains the integrity of their goals. Their ability to encapsulate ideas and feed those ideas back to others is appreciated by most and gives them the ability to navigate the formal and informal cultures of the organization and identify where processes need to be strengthened and systems developed. They then seamlessly integrate themselves where they are best utilized, often in non-traditional ways that they have specifically developed. Due to the value they place on communication and how deeply it is synthesized within their decision-making, they do not tolerate dishonesty among others and, as a result, they can seem inflexible, particularly since they are capable of being dishonest for the greater good and expect colleagues and subordinates to fall in line.

Handlers often are valued because they possess a blend of cooperation, caution, and combativeness. This ensures that they execute directions but stand ready to either inform superiors if they have concerns or go into battle on their behalf. This means they are able to effectively lead through transformation, reconciliation, or fear. They are direct and honest and therefore effective at managing up and down. They can do so with seemingly disparate messages and goals because, with the goal in mind, they focus on what their target needs to hear and understand. They handle both problems and opportunities with aplomb and, in short, they will save you from yourself by seeing both land mines and bridges where you might not. They also provide plausible deniability when saving you from yourself entails engaging a land mine or two. They will do the dirty work on your behalf for the good of the order. Because they are natural warriors, Handlers need to guard against disrupting process or the synergy of good work if they find cause to defend your honor or that of the company. In situations such as this, they can become overly passionate and distracting.

The Handler is a just-in-time learner and self-propelled actor. Handlers are in continuous personal improvement cycles of discovering and implementing so that they can act when the need arises. Since the Handler is often learning along the way and is a skilled listener who tends to details, their ideas are relevant, and they can identify a clear path to implementation. As a result, they will be inventive and open, meaning that a natural synergy comes about when they are working with other people. Handlers are able to come up with their own ideas, but they are most adept at building upon those of others and helping others do likewise.

TECHNIQUES TO MOTIVATE

Make sure to give Handlers space for thinking and devising. It is necessary, with all that they juggle, that they have the opportunity for peace and quiet as well as easy opportunities for one-on-one and small group discussions with members of their team. Do not use attendance or work hours as a method for motivation or performance assessment. That is an old school method that will not be successful with Handlers because they know that their effectiveness is tied to their relationships, not to their visibility. The Handler personality will be best motivated by short-term goals that involve tactical decisions and outcome management.

Handlers need to know they have support. They can become worrisome if they do not see it, and their natural courage could become fear. A Handler who does not think you have their back can become indecisive and look for ways to seek reassurance. This is not how you want them to spend their time. If you need to help coach them into different behavior, you should do this in a manner that is practical and to the point. Have your facts at hand and be ready to tell the Handler exactly what needs to change and why.

Because Handlers have a presence with decision-makers as well as with the rank and file, they have a good understanding of where there are disconnects and pain points in the organization. This allows them to develop perspectives and approaches that are both supportive to their multitude of stakeholders as well as realistic. Motivate them by ensuring they have open access to power. They tend to be inflexible and concerned with social status, so make sure they are honored with recognition and visible positions. Because of their dislike of uncertainties, they are likely to stay with an organization for a long time, so make sure to formally acknowledge their years of service.

Because the Handler is judgmental and combat-ready, it is a good idea to keep them involved in adversarial activities, even when small. When an argument must ensue, the Handler is your best bet for realizing victory. The Handler has the resolve and stamina to stay focused until the bitter end.

PLACE ON YOUR TEAM

Handlers are adept managers wherever you put them, but they are outstanding chief operating officers, corporate attorneys, and project managers. They are also effective as chiefs-of-staff and forepersons. They seek to build structure through security and, as such, their effectiveness is best used when they can polarize an argument or issue and then work through battle, compromise, and negotiation to get to a point of agreement. They are not particularly good at expressing emotions or recognizing that ability in others. Their concern for the facts can often cause them to ride roughshod over others.

When looking for employees who are natural Handlers, you want to look for individuals who are disciplined, logical, expressive, and quick to fight for themselves and what they believe in. They work hard, solve problems, and keep everyone informed. They value loyalty and will no doubt surround themselves with others who have similar respect for such ties.

Handler personality types are naturally reliable and conscientious with an eye to tradition. If you have this type of personality in your employee ranks, but there is not a management position available for them, give them stretch projects and make sure they know that you are doing so to improve them and better their opportunities. They are not likely to experiment and will, instead, stay the course. The Handler will be grateful for the grooming and mentoring, even if you both know another organization might eventually benefit. Your company still reaps the rewards immediately and, if they move on, you have created an ally out in the world. We all know that our networks come in handy for a multitude of reasons.

While the Handler personality may not have the vision that Captains have, they have more than their share of grit and are willing to take criticism and grow. As key members of your team, they can step-up to be situational leaders, even warriors for the cause. The combination of their internal locus of control with their need to be participatory ensures they will engage employees and successfully get them to listen and follow their directions.

EXAMPLES OF HANDLERS

Ruth Bader Ginsburg

Attorney, American Civil Liberties Union; professor, Rutgers Law School; Supreme Court Justice

Howard Schultz

CEO, Starbucks; owner, Seattle Super Sonics; co-founder, Maveron

Margaret Thatcher

Research chemist; barrister; Prime Minister, United Kingdom

THE ADVISOR

"It's going to rain, but we will all be fine."

PROFILE

The Advisor is an Ally who tends to be your best follower and your most loyal soldier. They are, as it is said, the ones who "drank the Kool-Aid®." These employees, regardless of their abilities, education, and skill level are loyal to both you and your organization and should, therefore, be fully utilized. They are trustworthy idealists. Without these dedicated workers, your business would go nowhere. They come to you ready to believe in you, the company mission, and the company's products and/or services. You do not have to earn their trust, but you can unearn it. Your goal is to ensure these employees are nurtured as well as informed. This requires some work on your part because nurturing requires you to dedicate time to reach out to these employees and informing requires providing digestible chunks of information. The information should be about you first so they come to know you and base their loyalty on your humanity, and about the organization second so they can spread the word about the good that is happening and the plans that are unfolding. Soldiers are very good at spreading the message through their actions as well as their words.

Advisors have a natural ability to intuit what others around them need and they hope to use this information to create balance and fairness. They have a high degree of emotional intelligence and insatiable curiosity so, if you have Advisors on your team, they can act as cultural glue bringing people and projects together in a way that plays to people's interests and natural inclinations. They are quite sure-footed, imaginative, and inventive, so they can work well with the Handler in determining where to plug people into processes and systems for optimal harmony. They are expressive and often act as cheerleaders when they are connecting people, which is why they must have a sense of you, as well as of your goals and the company's successes and goals. They are the Allies who spread your mission for you and connect people to it. Their compassion for others will help ensure that employees feel good about themselves and the company. They want to leave a mark on the world through comfort and kindness.

Because Advisors are so trusting, they can be risk-takers—often unintentionally. They are not always thinking of consequences; they are confident you and your leadership team are. They are certain things will turn out right and everyone will be taken care of. They are genuine and tend to assume everyone else is. They can be naïve. Be clear with Advisors regarding your expectations. They can become complacent and assume that results and positive outcomes are the result of attitude rather than hard work and performance. Keep them focused and believing in movement and incremental progress.

Because Advisors do their informal leading from a place of followership and natural advocacy, it is easy to forget that they need support as well. They are creative types who need the opportunity to express their individuality, not just their alignment to the organization. When you see that you have an Advisor, make sure that their uniqueness, passion, and creativity are honored, and that they don't lose themselves to the cause. This will ensure their longevity as your employee and keep them energized.

TECHNIQUES TO MOTIVATE

Advisors stay motivated when they feel appreciated and connected. Try to keep them somewhat in-the-know and seek their opinions whenever possible. Getting their perspectives will allow them to feel that their belief in you and the organization is well-founded, and it will also benefit you. Regardless of the rank or skill level of the Advisor, they will have valuable insight because they care enough to pay attention and to even be mindful of potential problems. This means your communication with them should be two-way. Seek them out for regular conversations.

The Advisor wants to make a difference, so you can motivate them by connecting them to activities that are altruistic. They would be happy to lead a fund drive for the organization or help guide the organization in charitable behavior, such as being green or socially responsible. This can also be parlayed into asking them to assist colleagues, such as being the supervisor of a stretch project or mentoring junior employees.

If you need to help an Advisor course correct, make sure to do that by brainstorming alternative pathways and by making it obvious to them how this ties into the big picture and their long-term goals.

Advisors are generally engaged, conscientious, and considerate, but it does not take much to cause them to swing to complacency and even carelessness. This can happen if they lose confidence in you, which can happen if they think you have lost your way. Simply put, they will stop believing in you if you stop believing in you. They are insightful and have the emotional intelligence to understand and cooperate with others, but it is rooted in their faith in you. They need to see you upholding the company values and mission, and if they see you slip morally, they need to see you respond with a *mea culpa* and an apology. They are a forgiving type, but only to those who seek forgiveness. This is crucial to understand because Advisors need to have someone to believe in. They have zealot tendencies. If you lose their support it will be hard to earn it back because their inclination to spontaneity will likely have driven them to seek a quick replacement for you.

PLACE ON YOUR TEAM

When you have Advisors who are highly educated and experienced, they often are publicists or directors of sales. As a chief marketing officer, the Advisor can effectively manage the reputation and branding of the entire organization. In a tribal sense, the Advisors fill the role of shaman or spiritual leader. Advisors can be placed anywhere you need diplomacy and advocacy. Because they are dedicated to eradicating inequality, they would make outstanding directors of diversity.

Advisors are the conscience of the organization. They keep you, and it, honest. Some can turn into zealots believing they know better than anyone else what is right and wrong and what inequities must be abolished. Advisors can be in management positions if their ideals align with that of the company, but you need as many Advisors as you can get, and a business cannot run with managers alone if it wants to expand. Advisors need to be sprinkled throughout your organization. You need them at the highest levels, but also among your backbone staff. Find honest, loyal, hardworking people and then cultivate and nurture them; or in other words, hire character and teach skills. But don't teach only skills. Drive your mission, enthuse your beliefs, inculcate your ethics, and be present and charming. Through this the Advisor will feel supported and want to reciprocate, not just through their work, but with their kind nature and sensitivity to the feelings of others.

Advisors seek to be engaged, but you have to engage them. Advisors are optimists who also are courageous, but they can burn out quickly. This makes them particularly valuable during a crisis or down-turn. Their need for a cause can be tapped in a situation where you need their hope and energy. But there needs to be an end in sight. They will sail the direction you want, if they see land ahead. They can help you pass on information in a positive light and solidify your support. But whether you are in good times or bad, they will serve you well as social media responders. They are also wonderful receptionists and executive assistants where their loyalty and belief can come together.

EXAMPLES OF ADVISORS

Reed Hastings

Member, California State Board of Education; co-founder and CEO, Netflix; philanthropist

Nelson Mandela

Attorney; anti-apartheid revolutionary; President, South Africa; Nobel Laureate

Malala Yousafzai

Human rights advocate; Nobel Laureate (youngest ever)

THE ENCOURAGER

"It's going to rain, but it will stop before there's a flood. And even if it floods, we'll have an ark built first."

PROFILE

The Encourager is an Ally and a strong and expressive communicator with a true ability to empathize. The Encourager is both emotionally intelligent and socially intelligent, and will use emotions to captivate and guide others. They do not listen as effectively as the Advisor, but they know how to parlay the beliefs of others into motivation and connect it to their own internal locus of control. In other words, they can be manipulative, but their reasons are generally noble. In their own moral system, the end justifies their means. More often than not, they are lifting and strengthening others.

The Encourager likes being in the know and connecting people to each other, facts, and concepts. Because of this, they will always have an opinion, and it is generally based on a preponderance of personally gathered evidence. If the Encourager is not sophisticated or intelligent, their knowledge can end up as company gossip. However, in the best-case scenario, a smart, savvy, and loyal Encourager brings out the best in others. Regardless of their position in the company, the Encourager will see it as a duty to reach many, if not all, others in the organization to ensure they know what is going on and have what they need to be successful. They are dynamic and inclusive.

The Encourager may be involved in many aspects of the organization and show up where needed but not always expected. They seem to have a sixth sense for where the action is and where they can be value-added. Encouragers are easy communicators, however, they do not like confrontation or arguments. They follow rules and authority and expect everyone else to as well. They are practical and efficient, but they also are a bit needy. They often drop in quickly with ideas and possible connections and disappear even more suddenly to avoid hearing why their idea might not be the best. Because the Encourager seeks out relationships across the organization, this can be problematic because they might pass on ideas before they are vetted and without hearing important criticism. It also is the case that the Encourager will intermingle their own ideas with those of leadership as they scatter information around, muddying the waters considerably. Keeping the Encourager on message is essential. Once they are on-message, they are adept at using their connections to get things done.

It is important to the Encourager that people feel taken care of. They are like the middle child who wants everyone to be happy, or at least operate in harmony. Encouragers will be quick to initiate a celebration and remember coworkers' birthdays and anniversaries. Some of this comes from a need to be liked, which also feeds their sense of humor and jovial personality. The Encourager is the person everyone likes, and while some will want to join them for drinks after work to find out what is going on at work, most will do so simply for fun. However, the Encourager can overwhelm more introverted types.

The Encourager is generally humble and finds satisfaction in building up others. The Encourager believes there is something for everyone and patiently helps other types seek out opportunities. They are cultural connectors who readily see what interpersonal connections could benefit the individuals with whom they work. Whether they are setting up colleagues on dates, suggesting a promotion to a manager, or pointing out the opportunity for carpooling to employees who didn't know they were neighbors, the Encourager wants everything to work the best it can for everyone.

The Encourager seeks to connect through belonging. Unfortunately, the Encourager is conflict avoidant and will either pull out comedic tendencies or claim ignorance if relationships go sideways or interfere with work performance.

TECHNIQUES TO MOTIVATE

Encouragers are highly conscientious, so they can be driven by messages, processes, or desired results. This makes them easily managed and monitored members of your team. However, they will feel most successful if they can see their influence in the company climate and don't feel that they are being overly scripted. Motivate them by giving them opportunities to influence the culture. They can conduct trainings or orientations, be a company ambassador, organize special events, lead peer committees, or help write policies.

Encouragers are highly cooperative, generally seeing and tending to an organizational need before it is brought to their attention. For that reason, they are often considered go-to people. One of the best ways to motivate them is to, indeed, go to Encouragers for assistance when you can and then show your appreciation by thanking and acknowledging them. They like to be influencers, so they will respond well to recognition, as long as it does not bring unwarranted attention or put them on the spot to publicly answer a question or develop an opinion. They are naturally engaged in the organization and in the lives of many employees, so the way to motivate is by helping them see and understand that what they are doing really matters. Since their energy is outgoing, they can be easily drained if you don't make an effort to fill them or have someone else fill them. They are conflict averse, and their feelings can also be easily hurt. Whatever you do, don't leave Encouragers to work in an isolated environment. That will demoralize them.

The Encourager seeks to feel loved and needed. This can be made real if they are flattered on a regular basis. They can be overly prideful, so it is not wise to do this continuously. If they are regularly flattered they risk feeling untouchable. This can result in them becoming manipulative and self-sacrificing in a way that is not beneficial to them or the organization. When the time comes to help the Encourager improve their behavior, it is best to focus on the value of the relationships they have and how a change could help boost their influence and, thereby, improve the organization.

PLACE ON YOUR TEAM

It is no surprise that Encouragers are popular. The Encourager is optimistic, approachable, and thrives in environments built on positivity. For that reason alone, it is beneficial to have them at several layers of your organization. They are a confidante and wingman and, because of their temperament, they would be great change agents. They will be dependable in devising tactics for communication and training and can easily instill confidence in others. However, they are not naturally strategic thinkers and will need to hear what your desired outcomes are for them and your planned strategies for the company.

Anywhere you need strong communication and someone who can organize people is a spot to consider placing an Encourager. They are strong middle managers who are good on your HR team–even as a chief human resource officer–or in tactical positions such as the writer of your newsletter. They will also be beneficial in a staff position, such as finance, human resources focused on development and training, or as a communications staff who can focus on policies, processes, and indoctrination.

The Encourager personality is nimble and can be placed in a variety of contexts, although they prefer to work in formal organizations with strict hierarchies. They have the skills to see the attributes of individuals and the complexity of individual problems. Placing this type of person where they can shepherd people would be wise. They are thoughtful and deliberate. If you find yourself in a situation where loyalty to you is suffering, mobilize your Encouragers and ensure they understand just what you need your employees to understand.

Their moods, especially joy and happiness, are contagious, so do what you can to make them happy. That said, if you have an Encourager whom you can't keep happy, or who plays favorites among the organization, it may be best to coach them out. This is particularly true if they are in a management position. They could end up leading people away from you if the path they are on is not aligned to you or your mission.

EXAMPLES OF ENCOURAGERS

Bill Clinton

Rhodes Scholar; attorney; Attorney General Arkansas; Governor, Arkansas; President, United States of America

Nancy Lublin

Founder, Dress for Success; CEO, Crisis Text Line; CEO, Do Something;

Sheryl Sandberg

Chief of Staff, United States Secretary of the Treasury; COO, Facebook; founder, LeanIn.org

THE ENABLER

"There will be a flood; do you want me to help build an ark or
teach others to build the ark?"

PROFILE

The Enabler is an Ally who is a quiet and effective communicator. Enablers trust their own intellectual skills quite well, and they
generally are right. The Enabler has some communication traits
similar to the Advisor and the Encourager, but they are not as
emotionally demonstrative. Because they are primarily observers
who listen carefully, they tend to understand situations with solid
objectivity. When this is combined with a natural ability to navigate
on an even keel, others feel comfortable seeking and taking their
advice. They quietly and steadily lead others and are seen as wise and
tempered. They fill the role of sage, guide, and oftentimes as the sto-
ryteller who imparts facts, entertains, or keeps others at arm's length.

While Enablers are effective, in part, because they have
emotional intelligence, they are not very emotional themselves,

even when driving action and results. They use their emotions to understand the needs of others, but they do not become sympathetic and, at times, not even empathetic. They are not hesitant to make tough decisions that might cause others discomfort or even harm. They can be rather Machiavellian, and they easily compartmentalize for business reasons. They also believe that, with the right training and guidance, others can become less emotional. They use their energy to drive efficiencies and personal performance outcomes.

The Enabler spends considerable time gathering, pondering, and disseminating facts. In order to do so effectively, they spend a great deal of time in reflection and reserved detachment. In a small organization, you can be sure everyone knows the Enabler and most people seek counsel from them. In larger organizations, employees will be familiar with the Enabler's reputation as someone to go to for help, support, or mentoring. While the Advisor is focused on ensuring people are happy, the Enabler is focused on ensuring people are trained and participating. They then sit back with faith in the employee's ability to engage the skills and knowledge to do what is necessary, when it is necessary.

Their diligence in doing the right thing with the available facts can cause Enablers to be overly confident and even blinded by their own egos. Since they see themselves as objective and others as swayed by emotion, they can be highly resistant to criticism about their behavior. When this is combined with a cold persona, the Enabler can inadvertently cut themselves off from needed information as a result of co-workers finding them unapproachable. However, when they do engage with colleagues, they get down in the trenches to create the staying power needed to see things through to the end.

Insatiable curiosity and a realistic approach to problem-solving are behaviors for which Enablers are appreciated. The Enabler approaches tasks with discipline and a clear process. When mentoring, Enablers enjoy imparting knowledge of how to transfer and scale processes. To an Enabler, the painstaking steps to goal achievement are the assurance it will happen. Enablers will be quick to ask to see a list of steps or flow charts to both understand and critique a current process.

Enablers are supportive of other people and able to lead through guidance or persuasion. They maintain control of themselves and their teams by ensuring information is shared appropriately and in a timely fashion. They are viewed by others as highly cooperative. This does not mean they look for consensus, however. They are adept at moving people calmly toward goals in a polite manner that is seen as collaborative even if those they are enabling don't see the realization of their own goals. Use your Encouragers when you want to change how your employees feel, but use your Enablers when you want to change how your employees behave. Employees who are viewed as objective and fact-based are able to influence the actions of others, in large part, because there is not a perceived message or action to fight against. The Enabler will deliver a message in a low-key manner.

TECHNIQUES TO MOTIVATE

Enablers work best in a culture of kindness where they and others can comfortably seek the truth. They tend to be personally reserved and expect others to be as well. They expect a high level of civility—probably because they find it easier to keep their emotions at bay if there are few reasons to become emotionally invested in a situation. For the Enabler, a culture of kindness also means time is allocated for reflection on progress and continuous evaluation of progress against core personal beliefs as well as against the organization's mission.

Enablers are comfortable in uncertainty, but only if they are able to adhere to a solid plan, preferably one they have created. They are inherently optimistic, but, in large part, it is because of their belief in themselves and their own creativity and resourcefulness. Enablers generally are current and attentive to what is trending—partly in hopes of leading the next trend. To get the most out of your Enablers, make sure they have the time and resources to develop plans and processes and the support from you and your leadership to formulate goals and deadlines based on the steps in their plans.

Friendly, though private, Enablers have a mentor's spirit and a love of teaching and training—whether it is formal or not. Their commitment to a tactical approach ensures that they can explain and contextualize strategies to others in meaningful ways that emphasize what each person can do. Your Enablers will thrive if they are able to spend time explaining things to other employees, and you will benefit as well since the Enabler is generally not able to go off-script. They seek the ideal through understanding.

Enablers are not going to want to stay with a company for very long unless they are upwardly mobile or can at least change departments or positions. They are easily bored, and when they are, they are not above taking risks or causing disruptions.

PLACE ON YOUR TEAM

Enablers are clever and adept at seeing what improvements are needed where. They are open-minded and tend to view situations and people from a logical perspective. They are able to step outside their own perspectives and view things without bias, and this makes them effective at getting people from point A to point B. However, they can be so dedicated to fact-finding and eliminating bias, they may find it difficult to devise a path to something completely different. In other words, their creativity is usually well contained and somewhat predictable. They also can become paralyzed by an inability to be swayed one way or another. However, this paralysis never happens in a time of crisis or urgency, so lean on them during these moments. It is essential that you surround your Enablers with Handlers and Advisors so that the Enablers are pushed into action and the Handlers and Advisors are supported with sufficiently neutral data and facts.

Enablers are explorers and examine the world through all of their senses, and they are comfortable with trial and error. Sometimes this is appropriate; sometimes they move too quickly or forget an important evaluation step as something new catches their interest. This means your logical, yet often spontaneous, junior Enablers should be supervised and have steps to follow. They like to be kept busy with a variety of work, so a good supervisor can keep them on-task and happy. Enablers don't provide emotional feedback and don't require it either.

Although they are permissive with themselves in the trial and error stage of figuring out a problem, their analysis of basic things can seem over-done, and their thoughtful consideration of details can seem like unnecessary pondering. You should have managers who are Enablers. How many depends upon the size of your organization. Enablers could be successful in higher managerial positions, but they are not likely to thrive unless they are doing fiscal and policy management. They would excel as scientists, engineers, graphic artists, and educators. They can be successful in the c-suite where they can blend routine and adrenaline, authority and risk-taking. They are competent chief academic officers, chief administrative officers, and chief information officers.

EXAMPLES OF ENABLERS

Warren Buffett

Securities analyst; Chairman and CEO, Berkshire Hathaway; philanthropist

Jaime Escalante

Math and physics teacher; subject of the book The Best Teacher in America and the film Stand and Deliver; co-winner, Peabody Award.

Wendy Kopp

Founder and president, Teach For America; CEO and Co-Founder, Teach For All

ASSOCIATES

THE INNOVATOR

"It's going to rain, and a flood is inevitable. Let's build a double-decker sailboat with solar panels."

PROFILE

The Innovator is an Associate who is ready to support you and your mission, but primarily they are dedicated to being creative and having an opportunity to pioneer an idea or product. They are curious and adaptable, and they don't want to be common or come up short when compared to others. They are guilty of spending considerable time in mental gymnastics or philosophical musings in order to solidify their reputation as people who operate differently and understand things on a more sophisticated level.

While it is important to Innovators to set themselves apart, they enjoy brainstorming with their colleagues and using them as part of their vetting process. Innovators are confident in their intellectual abilities, but they are continuous learners who readily grow from the ideas that emerge through contact with others. They are not, however, always confident in their conclusions, which is why they continuously vet their ideas and put off arriving at conclusions until the last minute. If allowed to, they will miss deadlines out of fear they have missed something in their investigation and analysis. They become so enmeshed in possibilities that they don't easily get out of their own heads and, instead, play a seemingly unending game of "what if."

They have the grit of a Captain, but they are more internally focused as they attempt to evolve ideas and opportunities into their grandest forms. As a matter of fact, many Innovators are introverts and will even appear shy around strangers or when they are asked to speak or present without advanced notice.

Innovators are able to gather information in many ways, but they are most skilled at intuiting how to solve a problem by coming up with unique combinations of small bits of logical analyses. They don't think in the linear fashion that often is assumed to go hand-in-hand with logical people. Instead, they chunk their logical conclusions into blocks of information that they can move around in uncommon ways. This can make it hard for other people to follow their reasoning because some of their connections don't naturally seem to work. This is the unique skill of the Innovator. They see what others don't, even when looking at all of the same pieces because the pieces are more free-floating.

Innovators are naturally supportive people who cooperate easily with others—probably because they have been fighting judgment of their uncommon approaches to problems—but they do not relate to people on an emotional level. They prefer to work things out from a rational and standoffish posture. Their need to view things differently and their comfort with being non-conformists can cause Innovators to undertake methods that can be seen by some as deviant. While most people will view them as open-minded, sometimes the Innovator's creativity combines with their skepticism to create irreverence. At times, this irreverence is a badge they wear; at other times, they don't even see it. Because of their adherence to logic, the Innovator can put together an argument to justify and defend anything as acceptable, including irreverent or disrespectful behavior. This can frustrate colleagues who see the Innovator as patronizing or dismissive. The Innovator, in turn, does not understand why they are seen as unsupportive when they are simply being honest.

As a result of strong imaginations and a steadfast dedication to meaningful outcomes, Innovators are natural entrepreneurs. They are willing to experiment with new processes and procedures and put considerable resources behind their visions. They will be courageous as they move forward, but there is a chance they are not considering potential alternative results. Their focus is not on unintended consequences or risk mitigation; they have their eyes on creation, invention, and the chance to make a difference.

TECHNIQUES TO MOTIVATE

Innovators desire to be unique in order to feel significant, and without assurances that they are, they can become melancholy. They can be caught up in envy, because they judge their own uniqueness by comparing themselves to others. You can effectively guide them by actively pulling them away from direct comparisons. Offer them critiques with specifics on how they might improve. Provide evidence and clear alternatives, and be ready to discuss possible alternative behaviors and outlooks.

Innovators are easily bored. Because Innovators are adept at listening to and observing others, it is easy to assume they are self-motivated. This is not necessarily the case. They need peace and quiet to be most effective, but they also need clear goals and opportunities to be inspired. While Innovators are disciplined and seek to fit in, they are introverts at heart and need space to incubate ideas. Once they have an idea, they are open in how and when they share it. So, while they don't readily engage with colleagues, they are engaged with organizational goals, and this can be leveraged to help drive their effectiveness and utilized to motivate other employees.

Innovators like to create structure and they are always seeking to make things better. This means they are particularly motivated by pushing perfection toward simplicity and vice versa. They are abstract thinkers who have the ingenuity to see the potential for helpful improvements to the most basic products and processes without overly complicating things. They see patterns and therefore discrepancies. This is where much of their creativity arises. Nurture their enthusiasm and natural problem-solving abilities to motivate and encourage them. They do not take criticism well, so it is best to sandwich negative comments between comments pointing out what you value about them. You will get the most out of them this way.

PLACE ON YOUR TEAM

Innovators prefer adaptive work to standard work. They are not at their best in jobs that are focused on day-to-day activities and the maintenance of the status quo. Many people with the spirit of the artist, such as the Innovator, are caught up in the process of creating and not as focused on the results. Lucky for you, the Innovator cares about results and making things work for the bigger picture. They are able to be both planful and spontaneous, and their ingenuity, in large part, emerges from this shared space. They take the time and patience to develop concepts and schemas, and when their ideas have come together, they are like Archimedes yelling, "Eureka!" through the streets. Their perspective is creative, but their approach is conscientious and exacting. It usually is their confidence in their abilities that marries these attributes effectively. It is essential they find ways to bolster their confidence so it is always on hand. They are doers, not explainers, so having them show results or models, rather than paths and processes, will help others see what is evident to them.

Innovators cannot be employed anywhere on your team. They need to be in positions where they can use their creativity to advance the organizational mission, expand revenue streams, or create new offerings. If not properly placed in your organization, they can be insensitive and even condescending as they take out their frustrations and lack of empathy on those around them. They are entrepreneurs who spend time imagining what the future could hold for the organization if things were done differently. They work best alone, or in pairs, on projects they find meaningful.

They value honesty and integrity and are best placed in your research department, but they could be very successful in product development, technology, business analysis, or corporate strategy.

In your C-suite, an Innovator who is experienced in considering the feelings of others before pulling the trigger on decisions can be a strong chief technology officer.

EXAMPLES OF INNOVATORS

Neil deGrasse Tyson

Astrophysicist; Director, Hayden Planetarium; television personality

Tiera Guinn

Aerospace engineer; design engineer, Boeing; lead engineer, Space Launch System, NASA

Hedy Lamarr

Actor; producer; inventor of Spread Spectrum Technology

THE PLANNER

"It's going to rain, and I have a policy and process to build an ark, and we can sell it to a cruise line when the floods recede."

PROFILE

The Planner is an Associate who can take even the most complex theory or complicated idea and mold it into actionable strategies and tactics by refining the core details and issues. They are a perfect conduit between abstract thinkers and the workers who have to implement their ideas. If you find yourself wanting to ask someone, "Do you need me to draw you a picture?" you probably need to bring in a Planner who can translate big pictures into small ones and lofty goals into actionable parcels. Planners may or may not be introverts, but they will quietly approach their work and share thoughts only as necessary.

Planners are naturally decisive, but they are not impulsive. They base their decisions on observation, logic, analysis, and well thought out conclusions. They have a thirst for knowledge, so their knowledge-base is usually current and equal in depth and breadth. They are conscientious in ensuring the right people have input in decisions they make and premises they form. They exhaustively vet their ideas before going on to apply their findings.

They are quick to self-correct and correct others, but that is not often necessary. The Planner ensures that foundations are set, and roadmaps are complete, and they do so from a strong self-assured persona that builds trust and followers. For the Planner, nothing is created by accident or utilized randomly, and that includes people and their ideas. The Planner can be a ready disciplinarian, if necessary, but does so with an open mind and the goal of finding the win-win.

Planners work diligently and will prove to be prolific in whatever they endeavor to produce, whether products, ideas, or schematics. Their approach is strategic, but they are highly imaginative and valuable in coming up with new processes. They are realistic and care deeply about outcomes. When they are instrumental in driving an operational plan, they are cautious and able to mitigate unintended consequences.

Regardless of their position in the organization, Planners are seen as the boss or at least bossy. They are confident to the point of being judgmental, but this allows them to make quick decisions that anchor others. They can appear cold and calculating, so their efficient and intellectual approach is not appreciated by everyone. They are level-headed, but their insatiable curiosity causes them to question pretty much everything, leading some to question their loyalty. Planners are loyal to the organization and the mission and they will seek opportunities to grow both. They do not naturally support conventions and traditions. This can frustrate colleagues and annoy superiors, particularly if they go after the organization's mission, vision, or values. Fortunately, Planners are discerning and have a passion for dignity. They will keep debate at a high level and walk away from gossip. Planners are also conflict averse, so disagreements are short-lived.

Planners can appear nervous, due to their fear of letting people down or, more importantly, missing a variable or dependency. They may incessantly seek reassurance from subject-matter experts that they are on the right track and have all of the required information and facts. Their diligence is quickly prized as colleagues come to realize they listen carefully and respect the part everyone plays in putting together the optimal road to success. They communicate in a rational, direct style that is broadly appreciated even when it does not align with social or corporate norms. The confidence of the Planner, with a generous sprinkling of charisma, affords them a fair amount of leeway with colleagues. Managers will value the Planner's ability to critique their ideas in a fair, rational, and objective manner while still being provocative enough to force essential self-reflection and critical analysis.

TECHNIQUES TO MOTIVATE

Don't waste their time with feel-good meetings or team-building exercises. Planners enjoy being experts in their field, and you will get the most out of them if they are given latitude to explore their interests and develop competencies in areas they desire knowledge and skill. Provide them with clear direction and get out of their way. Then, deliver any necessary criticism with facts and rationale. Make sure they can see the fruits of their labor. Planners are driven by success so they need to see things to fruition and beyond.

Planners are hardworking and determined to be successful at all they attempt. They will work hard and put in the hours needed to accomplish their goals—which often are loftier than necessary. They generally are successful at reaching their goals because they put in the time, reduce redundancies, and co-opt colleagues. To motivate them, make sure they have a sufficient number of people to have influence over. These can be people in their vertical, or members of a team where it is commonly understood the Planner is the greater among equals. When you suggest ways they might improve, make sure to present schemas, and be ready for a later discussion, with specifics, as to why the Planner needs to change.

You can best motivate the Planner by putting them in positions where they can tackle intellectual challenges with little or no micro-managing. Surround them with people who share their values, such as the need to be goal-focused and efficient. They thrive in solitary work or with others similarly focused on creating the best. They are not appreciative of their more social colleagues or those who believe their work is "good enough." Planners find both of these attitudes foster a form of laziness. They are cooperative, but they will be critical of colleagues who do not share their work ethic, so it is best to place them with like-minded people or allow them to work remotely or in relative seclusion.

PLACE ON YOUR TEAM

Planners need to be isolated from unnecessary interruptions—keeping in mind that they would probably define all interruptions as unnecessary. Believe it or not, you probably have a senior level position for which all of the above would be okay, especially when filled by a Planner who is a natural leader.

They can be effective managers because they are quite respectful and open to change that is presented with a logical argument. They are not beholden to a hierarchy and prefer to earn respect through hard work and dedication to impartiality and equality. As a matter of fact, Planners can accomplish much through their willpower and strength of convictions, not to mention the force of their personalities.

They like to reward their employees for hard work and initiative the same way they like to be rewarded for it. They believe anything is possible if you try hard enough. They also believe most people won't try hard enough; therefore, they only fully trust themselves. Those who cannot keep up with the morality and work ethic of the Planner will quickly lose their respect. This arrogance can alienate people at times, and, unfortunately, you will probably have to coach the Planner to care more about the importance of engaging the knowledge and skills of others.

Since Planners are apt to make unilateral decisions after treating disagreements as chess games to be won, it makes sense to place the smartest Planners in senior management positions where they can take their commitment to perfection and subject matter expertise to the highest levels.

The Planner is competent in any senior management position, including the C-suite. In lower positions, they will run into problems with supervisors who are not secure and intelligent. The Planner is able to quickly grasp new concepts and develop new competencies, impressing some and annoying others. The Planner will claim expertise in short order regardless of how deep their knowledge goes. This is because the Planner knows that with enough knowledge, intellect, common sense, and ability to persuade, they can make good decisions and create a following as well. Planners make good project managers, architects, analysts, and strategists.

EXAMPLES OF PLANNERS

Jennifer Doudna

Biochemist; professor, University of California, Berkeley; investigator, Howard Hughes Medical Institute; developer of CRISPR technology

Colin Powell

General, United States Army; National Security Advisor; Chairman of the Joint Chiefs of Staff; Secretary of State

Bill Gates

Founder, Chairman and CEO, Microsoft; philanthropist; humanitarian

THE EXECUTOR

"There will be a flood, and I will ensure an ark is built. I already have bids out to the best shipbuilders."

PROFILE

The Executor is an Associate and represents the typical hero who seeks to save the day. Executors seem to be always trying to prove themselves, but it usually is because they are not certain they are doing enough. They want to make a difference in a way that allows them to leave their mark. They want to save others, change the world, or improve the organization by making a significant difference.

Executors are duty-bound and will appear to be searching for something and eagerly seeking to answer a call. To fellow employees, they are someone to admire. They are self-sufficient, exciting, and add a flare to all they do. Their focus is usually on something others support which emboldens their colleagues. They are quick learners and superb multitaskers who want to succeed on their own merits. They invest their energy in the present and will take responsibility for their mistakes. They are resourceful and clever, adept at maintaining control, and getting themselves, and others, out of trouble.

The Executor is highly competitive, and although they can appear as the protagonist in your organization's story, they care just as much about going after a personal best—whether in the way of a title or scope of responsibility. Still, they are fiercely loyal and conscientiously results-driven. Their effortless use of power and ability to tolerate discomfort gives them staying power and makes them a worthy opponent or ferocious ally. To a nemesis, they provide energetic resistance; to a friend, they provide safety and inspiration.

Executors are natural teacher-leaders who often are called upon by others to step up and lead from an instructional or servant-leader standpoint. Sometimes this is a formal promotion, sometimes this is an informal result of followers thrusting them up. Either way, Executors will use their allure and political savvy to gain followers, and they will keep those followers through their commitment to helping people learn all that they can learn and achieve all the goals they desire. Guiding others and challenging them to be their best is their sweet spot, so they often cultivate other leaders easily, naturally, and in a transformational manner.

Even though their big and bold personalities can be too much for some people, the Executor is often able to use their charisma to guide, if not co-opt others. They do this from their natural belief in the right of all employees to have a voice and influence in their environment. Besides, they are personable and likable. Because of their belief in people and everyone's ability to rise to moral convictions, Executors are tolerant of the mistakes or misunderstandings of others. They simply believe that people are missing information, not an ability to arrive at the right conclusion, and they definitely believe there is a "right" conclusion. They are not very tolerant of their own mistakes and foibles, which makes them amazingly reliable. Whether they agree with you or not, Executors will put aside their own ideals long enough to rise to the occasion and meet organizational goals. If they are not able to do so because of the dissonance between organizational beliefs and their own beliefs, they will simply move on to a more compatible organization.

Executors are effective, in large part, because they are kind, reliable, competent, and, therefore, trusted. Within organizations, employees compare notes, and the Executor fares well in such conversations. As a result, their reputation improves exponentially. Of course, under an insecure supervisor, this populist leadership can seem threatening as it can almost appear as a cult or fan club. Additionally, average employees can find it difficult to find the energy to keep up with the charisma and passion of the Executor.

TECHNIQUES TO MOTIVATE

Executors are people people who truly enjoy interacting with others and getting to know them beyond a superficial level. Since Executors trust the beliefs and experiences of other people, this is a good starting point for finding ways to motivate them. They will seek ways to create authentic experiences for the people in their vertical if not all people in the organization. If you can tap into the altruistic bent of the Executor, you will enable them to accomplish great things. While it's lovely to believe that all employees are well-meaning and capable of looking after the interests of the organization, this is not entirely true, even if true to the Executor. Therefore, the enthusiasm the Executor has for the aptitude for others likely needs to be tempered.

It is essential to the Executor that they make a difference, and it is even more important that this difference has legs. They are motivated by knowing there is a legacy to their work—that the benefit of their efforts will be ongoing. They seek to inspire others and make them feel special. If the Executor is not living up to your standards, you can easily help them pivot by discussing with them how a change will have long term improvement potential. It is essential to them that their work is meaningful and connected to their personal values. The weaker this connection, the less engaged the Executor will be.

Executors can appear to be motivated by the greater good, but that does not mean they are immune to feeding their own self-worth. Being appreciated for their good work and noble goals is extremely important to them. Executors also can fall into the trap of being people pleasers, and as a result, they will take on extra work—sometimes work that rightfully belongs to others. To ensure you are properly motivating them, it is a good idea for you to keep an eye on their workloads and to help ensure that they are not taken advantage of. Demonstrate your appreciation of them by pointing out how they are reaching their own goals. They are most motivated by their own ideals and can lose confidence if they do not live up to their own expectations.

PLACE ON YOUR TEAM

Executors are emotional and comfortable with the emotions of others. This can cause them to be either beautifully empathetic or highly distracted as they become ensnared in the personal lives of subordinates or colleagues. While they have strong emotional intelligence, they do not always set boundaries to protect their time and heart. If they are managers, you can count on them to motivate their employees through both meaningful activities and symbolic gestures. They may need some coaching, though, when it comes to personnel matters in which they could rely too heavily on their belief in the goodwill and redemptive abilities of others instead of facts and concrete behavior.

They are optimists who believe in making a difference in society, not just in the organization, so they are most effective in organizations that can tie these together. If you can speak to their concern for a better world, and show how your organization improves lives, you will get the most out of an Executor. They are mission driven.

Executors have strong personalities and talent for winning over others and de-escalating tense situations. They are known for this and are pleased to stake their reputation on it. Use your Executor where you need political clout or a group of people assuaged. But keep in mind that they can drive other people beyond their capabilities thereby putting others or the organization at risk. They are well-aware of their own strengths and shortcomings, but they tend to overestimate the gifts and talents of others.

Executors are awesome wherever you might need a diplomat.

They can find the greater good and the best compromise, but they are skittish when they have erred. Criticism is hard for them, and they could resort to manipulation to resolve the dissonance. They are natural managers wherever they are, but they prefer to be placed where they see themselves helping to provide a greater good to more people. Executors make strong government relations directors, HR administrators, customer service managers, fundraisers, event coordinators, team leads, and instructors. If yours is a not-for-profit organization, or one that is dedicated to improving lives, Executors can be extraordinary executive directors.

EXAMPLES OF EXECUTORS

Tim Cook

Industrial engineer; CEO, Apple

Pope John Paul II

Helped end communism in Europe; Canonized by the Catholic Church

Oprah Winfrey

Talk show host; actor; media executive; producer; philanthropist

THE INVESTIGATOR

"There will be a flood, and I've built myself a little boat to
weather the storm."

PROFILE

The Investigator is an Associate who has great integrity and will be
among your most responsible and accountable employees. They are
strong analysts who tend to be conscientious and serious by nature
and come through when needed with a no-nonsense approach.
Investigators will find the answer needed or solve the problem
at-hand. Once they believe they have the right answer or correct
approach, they can be stubborn and closed-minded, but because
their solutions generally are right, this attitude often elicits more
eye-rolls than arguments.

Although they are detail-oriented and will research all the facts
before making a decision, Investigators are quick and resolute
decision makers. They seek to understand all points of view, but
they are realistic in their assessment of situations and conservative

in their approach to problem-solving, at times even nostalgic. Investigators seek order and predictability and prefer to keep things safe. As a result, they are orderly, process-driven, rule followers. The Investigator's by-the-book attitude has its place in every organization, although it needs to be tempered by those who understand that company policies may need to be re-evaluated if they are contrary to strategic goals or affecting revenue.

Investigators appreciate accountability, so they readily take responsibility for themselves and their team. They often are valued because they will not make assumptions or make estimates. It is important to them that what they say or predict is as accurate as possible. They have a sense of duty to the organization as well as to correct behavior. Their perspective is appreciated by colleagues, but because the Investigator is often disassociated and aloof, their behavior is not always understood and welcomed. Investigators see themselves as objective and probing, but others often consider their reservations and detachment more negatively and might think of them as too suspicious of others if not downright paranoid. In most situations, Investigators trust themselves more than others, although they can quickly be enamored of those in power. They admire positional power, and since they are not very ambitious themselves, they tend to look in awe at those who have navigated the company hierarchy.

Investigators value traditions and are committed to creating long-term, if not lifetime, careers for themselves. If you treat the Investigator with respect and provide them with the right level of autonomy, they will make your organization their home and prove to be a reliable and valuable employee. They need space, both literally and figuratively, and so the Investigator easily slips into the organizational background. As a result, those who don't know the Investigator certainly will see them as introverted and may see them as naïve due to a calm demeanor that is slow to anger. Also, it is not important to the Investigator to be cool or culturally current, so they may appear less sophisticated than they are simply due to the measuring stick being used. Investigators simply want to be happy.

Because they spend so much time alone, there is a danger the Investigator could forego real life experiences for an existence among concepts and ideals. The benefit of this penchant is that they tend to remain objective when analyzing things and don't get emotionally invested. The downside is that they have fewer experiences to draw from. Investigators take the road well-traveled and have a limited worldview. They don't know what they don't know but they assume their analyses and conclusions are correct. As a result, Investigators guard their beliefs and can become stingy with their ideas and processes, assuming that others should share their perspective and be equally self-sufficient in seeking results. This misjudgment often comes from not understanding that people have various ways of knowing and preferred ways of expressing.

TECHNIQUES TO MOTIVATE

It is important to Investigators that they achieve a level of mastery, and they are fearful of being helpless or incapable. Investigators are motivated by milestones and timelines and can be disillusioned, if not angered, by those who cannot adhere to deadlines, or worse yet, get in the way of meeting theirs. Investigators also care deeply about laws, rules, and ethics. Try to demonstrate to them how such things are important to you, and do not expect them to cut corners or look the other way. They are apt to report mistakes and infringements of others for the sake of the organization and righteousness. They really just want to be happy and content, and they believe this happens more readily in a controlled environment where they feel emotionally safe and secure—although whether this is the case or not is not always apparent.

Because of their dedication to doing what is right, they are quite valuable in positions where they provide you and others with honest feedback or objective assessments. Placing them in positions where they can help write an employee handbook or code of ethics, or where they can help develop or analyze and climate survey, will keep them engaged and feeling positive about the organization.

Investigators are committed to meeting deadlines and milestones. Therefore, Investigators can burn out quickly due to their willingness to sacrifice their personal lives for the organization and desire to stay with the same organization for many years. You can help keep your Investigators functioning well by making sure they are taking the time off they have earned and deserve, and that they don't push unrealistic deadlines on themselves and the team. When the Investigator needs more of a critique, make sure that you are quick and to the point. Be practical with your examples and give the Investigator time to process and then come back to discuss possible changes.

PLACE ON YOUR TEAM

Due to their conviction to all things practical and logical, and their propensity to analyze everything to exhaustion, the Investigator is particularly successful in research or investigation, regulatory compliance, legal affairs, and security. They are also strong financial auditors and accounting clerks. Basically, they are good employees in positions that follow tradition and in environments that don't change often. They prefer positions with clearly defined roles and duties. Investigators will meet deadlines and probably do so coming in under budget by incorporating new efficiencies. They take promises very seriously, and you can trust their word. You cannot, however, expect them to add creativity or innovative strategies to the mix. It is not their strength.

Investigators want things to be orderly, and they are not patient. They work best where they do not have to abide laziness, inattentiveness, or indecisiveness. They tend to keep their heads in facts, so they do work well with those who can add shading to their concepts by understanding and adhering to the underlying principles in play. Investigators generally are not successful managing others because they see things as black or white, can be hyper-critical, and lack empathy. They will not consider the feelings of co-workers, but seasoned Investigators will likely have learned to at least feign caring and team members will appreciate their calmness and sense of duty. Ironically, they do not respond well to criticism, particularly when given face-to-face, so it is best to correct their deficiencies in writing with examples and explanations as to why the behavior hinders organizational success. Then follow-up with a face-to-face conversation when the Investigator is prepared to respond.

Don't be surprised if your Investigator just wants to work alone.

Not having to rely on others appeals to the Investigator's need to control their work environment. Investigators don't like to feel as if they need others. They need facts and data; needing another person can seem like failure to them. Additionally, Investigators like to prove themselves, and this is much harder to do when producing reports or products as a team-member.

EXAMPLES OF INVESTIGATORS

Albert Einstein

Theoretical physicist; developer of the Theory of Relativity; led the Manhattan Project

Huateng "Pony" Ma

Founder, chairman and CEO, Tencent; deputy, 5th Shenzhen Municipal People's Congress; serves in the 12th National People's Congress

Maria Montessori

Physician; educator; founder of the Montessori Method; special education advocate

THE DEFENDER

"It always rains and never floods. If it does, we can go to higher ground and wait for rescue."

PROFILE

The Defender is an Associate who is tempered in both perspective and approach. The Defender is not a pessimist or an optimist; the Defender is a realist who points out the good and the bad with equal measure, free of hyperbole and unnecessary emotion. They help ground and guide others from a calm, caring disposition. They simultaneously see the mission and values of the organization as well as those of the individual employees. This enables them to ferret out discord and bring people together around common goals that are not generally obvious to others.

Defenders are open to changes and improvements, but they will insist on seeing the supporting data or even conducting an analysis themselves. This goes for any changes that need to be made to their own personality or behavior, as well. If you need the Defender to improve or change behaviors, you will need to be friendly and open about it, providing data while also stressing the importance of joint loyalty. If the argument for change is not compelling, they will not embrace it. They prefer the status quo.

From their very core, Defenders want to make a difference and help people, and even though they have an eye for data, they are more motivated by their sense of caring. They are nurturers who seem to have an instinct to pull the team together in a familial way. They will jump in if they sense they are needed, even before necessary analysis has taken place. They tend to be particularly kind. This is not just because of their altruistic nature, but also because they are clever enough to know that making a difference in the lives of others is more effective when made from a foundation of respect and warmth.

Defenders resist openly challenging others, but they are quick to protest something not substantiated. Defenders are skeptical, and can go overboard with denying what others embrace. In addition to denying a problem exists, there is a risk that the Defender will deny positive results and forecasts. The Defender's goal is not to predict gloom and doom, but to be seen as the one who has the answers. Sometimes this means they want to be seen as more informed than you. They don't see this as disloyal. They want to be trusted and seen as having access. They take great pride in their loyalty to, and defense of, the organization. However, combined with their confidence, this can lead to them inadvertently usurping your authority. Some colleagues might see them as transparent and trying to make you transparent. Defenders might even appear more credible than you if they have been with the company longer, or if they are highly intelligent. They will be quick to point out things that have happened in the past, even if the context is not the same. Your memory, or that of their immediate supervisor, will need to be sharp in order to respond on point. Defenders are dedicated and sincere, so getting them back on track—or into their own lane—is as easy as pointing out your concern.

Defenders are meticulous and efficient and seek to connect all aspects of the organization in order to strengthen it. They naturally work against silos because they are able to imagine the synergy that can come from not-yet-made connections. They easily see the big picture and where people can be plugged in because of their personalities and skills, and they take pride in helping employees find their voice and value in the organization. Defenders will help put structures in place and lead teams the way a conductor leads an orchestra.

TECHNIQUES TO MOTIVATE

Defenders are hard-working with a proclivity for allegiance. If you build on their natural inclination to support the organization and put them into roles where they can actively buoy others, their loyalty to you will build. Their inner life is important to them, so Defenders look for rules by which to set their internal compass. They may be religious or spiritual, or actively participate in groups rooted in common values and philosophies. Recognizing this, in a manner appropriate to your organization, can inspire and fuel them. This is important because Defenders rely on an internal locus of control more than external, so ensuring they have opportunities to keep themselves balanced will pay off for the organization.

They seek to make sense of their own lives through service. They want to make life easier for others, and at work this means they thrive in helping colleagues solve problems, meet deadlines, and improve quality. They may seem dedicated to the status quo, but only so far as it supports themselves and their fellow employees. They do not like change for the sake of change, but they can comfortably move in a different direction and take progressive steps if it serves a greater good. Make sure Defenders are connected to your mission. To further solidify their loyalty to you and the organization, make sure they are also connected to any worthy causes your organization takes on.

Defenders are results driven, but they are detached from those giving praise or coaching. They want outcomes to speak for themselves. For that, they enjoy appreciation and generally assume it. So, although they will be quick to compliment and praise others, Defenders don't really care if you are proud of them. They want to know you think they and what they do matter. Reward their work privately and sincerely, and refrain from comparing them to others, which will make them feel self-conscious and guilty. They are not motivated by your emotions; they are motivated by their own influence. This is what makes them go above and beyond. However, although they are not motivated by others' emotions, they are cognizant of them and empathetic as well. They use this awareness to creatively support others and offer advice.

PLACE ON YOUR TEAM

Defenders are sure and steady and will welcome any task that moves a project or process toward the desired goal. They will not complain that they are bored or underutilized. They will do what is needed from where they are placed. They make good team leaders who will shepherd all projects through to completion. They will often subordinate their own needs for the group, so it is important to manage them in a way that ensures their needs are articulated and met. Family matters to them, so they will seek positions where there is sufficient work-life balance.

Defenders seek win-win scenarios, so they are good in situations where negotiations are needed, and it is important that all parties walk away feeling as if they have been heard and their needs at least partially met. They can be naïve, so it is important that you are clear with your expectations. You will be helping them enormously if you can advise them on the games and manipulation they can expect in business.

The best positions for Defenders are those that allow them to support others. They are outstanding in human resources, but can be valuable as assistants, coordinators, customer service representatives, and as technical support or help desk operators. As managers, they are particularly beneficial with young or inexperienced team members who need coaching and continuous feedback. Because they are empathetic and naturally remember facts about others, they are effective in sales where they eagerly give red-carpet treatment and can make clients feel as if they are part of a family. If you are operating a community service or healthcare organization, you will find that Defenders will successfully fulfill any position because of their bond with your mission. As higher-level managers, Defenders are approachable and lead in a democratic, if not servant-leader, manner.

EXAMPLES OF DEFENDERS

Sir Fazle Hasan Abed

Founder and Chair Emeritus, BRAC; appointed Knight Commander of the Most Distinguished Order of St. Michael and St. George

Eric Greitens

Rhodes Scholar; Navy Seal; awarded the Bronze Star and Purple Heart; founder, The Mission Continues; Governor, Missouri.

Strive Masiyiwa

Founder and Executive Chair, Econet Wireless; member, Africa Progress Panel (APP); humanitarian.

ACCOMPLICES

THE DISRUPTOR

"It's going to rain, and I built a self-contained living
space fueled by water."

PROFILE

The Disrupter is an Accomplice who looks at the world differently. They bring a spark of genius to a team looking to do things in an innovative way or solve problems that have befuddled others. They are proud of their cleverness and resourcefulness and enchanted by the idea of tackling the seemingly impossible. The Disruptor's chief talent is an ability to turn disadvantages into advantages and redeploy unusable processes or products in a different form.

Disruptors are filled with contradictions. They are well-informed, but they can't help getting in their own way. Although they thrive on changing things through agitation, it often is their mercurial personality itself that rattles their colleagues and the status quo. One day they are quiet and subdued, the next day they are charming and supportive, and the next they are provocative and insulting.

Disruptors are curious, imaginative, and creative. These traits are appealing to their managers, and with their out-of-the-box thinking, they do not have trouble obtaining work. They are difficult employees because they enjoy experimenting with anything—particularly social norms. They challenge social conventions and relish upsetting the status quo and those attached to it. This means they will rub many people the wrong way, but with the right sense of humor, they can quickly ease that pain and advance their agenda. They are not callous however. They care about the feelings of others and are fairly sensitive to the emotions around them. They might seek to minimize conflict almost as soon as they have created it, but only as it helps to serve their needs. Conflict is a tool they use to keep others off guard, gain attention to their argument, beat down enemies, and bolster a negotiating position.

Disruptors see themselves as catalysts and necessary for the growth of the organization. Their goal is to free themselves and the organization from non-essential constraints. Unfortunately, because of their reputation for combativeness, they generally are not in the same rooms as decision-makers and, therefore, are completely unable to determine what is or is not an essential constraint. They are planful, but when it comes down to making decisions, they rely too heavily on their intuition. And, while they seek to be change agents, their lack of discipline can leave them more as rabble rousers.

Imagination is something that drives the Disruptor and helps them shake things up. They want to quench their own thirst and, in the process, they often are able to capture the attention of others as they take a bold path toward their vision. Their adventurous spirit and courage in throwing themselves into the mix can captivate employees at all levels, but in a relative short period of time, their carelessness and lack of follow-through becomes apparent and may be viewed as unacceptable. They are like the proverbial fire that burns hot and fast.

Disruptors are confident in their own abilities, which energizes them and drives a high level of optimism. When it comes to others though, they tend to be suspicious and pessimistic. In fact, their manipulation of others is rooted in their belief that it really doesn't matter because others lack the needed talent. They truly do not see the value that others bring to the table, at least as far as developing strategies or advancing the ball. This does not mean that they take full responsibility or rush into things. They are judicious with timing and shrewd in their approach. They are independent, efficient, and use emotional expression to get the attention they need to ensure their voice is heard.

Because they notice and adroitly respond to emotions, they are able to influence the actions of others by creatively playing on their feelings in order to advance their own agenda. Their creativity often expresses itself in artistic ventures, so Disruptors either use their talent to advance their goals or to distract others away from opposing goals. Likely to infuse their imagination, Disruptors prefer to delve into that which satisfies their curiosity.

TECHNIQUES TO MOTIVATE

Ruled by their emotions, most Disruptors have found ways to cope with their tempers and passions. They can blend into the background unless something sparks their interest, at that point they can become shockingly passionate. They seek power in order to change the way things are, so they are highly motivated by advancement. This can be in the form of control, title, or wealth. If, on the other hand, you need to stop the Disrupter from certain behaviors, this is best done through a practical approach that is calm, friendly, and focuses both on the good and the bad. Be sure the Disruptor knows that their relationship with you is okay and that you recognize their underlying loyalty to the organization, even when it is not apparent.

The goal of a Disruptor is to build a sense of identity through their work and experiences. They will focus first on how they matter and second on your specific goals. It is essential that you guide them in seeing how they matter to the mission, and better yet, to the bottom line. If they are not properly guided, or if they do not see how they fit into a situation or the overall strategies through their day-to-day work, they can become frustrated and shut down.

Focusing on the here and now and short-term goals is a strength of Disruptors, so it is best to make sure the team they are on is balanced by a sufficient number of members who are focused on long-term goals and strategies. Disruptors work best in enriched environments where they have flexibility and an opportunity to shine. They will not do well if they are micromanaged or second-guessed. Doing things because "they have always been done this way" is not going to appeal to them. Disruptors bring fresh eyes to a problem regardless of how long they have been with the organization or in their position.

PLACE ON YOUR TEAM

Disruptors are unpredictable and, therefore, hard to manage, but they bring an ingenious lens to problems. They are bold thinkers who may offend some people and rock the boat, but with the right people tempering them and challenging them, their ideas can meld into something that positively disrupts your business, and maybe even an entire industry. If their idea or product is one that appeals to a broader customer base, you have struck gold.

The independence that is foundational to the Disruptor can cause uneasiness in those who are not comfortable with their unpredictability, spontaneity, and live-in-the-now perspective. Additionally, their competitiveness can make them seem as if they seek only accolades with little regard for others. This is not true. Disruptors are disassociated, but they are happy to share the glory. They just don't have the skills to do it well or ascertain the best timing.

Disruptors often are risk-takers and most satisfied with a bellicose approach. They want to bring chaos to ideas and processes, so it is good for them to have plenty of opportunities to be alone with their thoughts and ideas with time to try out concepts on colleagues. Their creativity is rooted in solitude, although it is in your best interest to have others step in and out of their territory to ensure they are not missing deadlines or ignoring unintended consequences. Find positions for the Disruptor that resemble project management and consulting work. Help them concentrate their natural inclination toward shock and awe to short term goals that need a boost of sideways thinking.

Positions where Disruptors can shine include working as sole contributors without direct reports, project managers where they can concentrate on goals with short timeframes, staff positions where their creativity can spark the work of others, and creative positions where they can engage their senses, tap into their imaginative sources, and share their eagerness to improvise.

EXAMPLES OF DISRUPTORS

Amelia Earhart

Pilot; aviation pioneer; adventurer

Jane Goodall

Primatologist and anthropologist; expert on chimpanzees; founder, Jane Goodall Institute; named a Dame Commander of the Most Excellent Order of the British Empire

Jeff Weiner

CEO, LinkedIn

THE PREACHER

"There might be a flood, but we can build an ark with prayer and
divine guidance."

PROFILE

The Preacher is an Accomplice who loves to argue and enjoys
even more the opportunity to tear apart the arguments of others.
The consummate devil's advocate, the Preacher will egg on anyone
to either make a point, argue a point, or fill the time. While they
often are concerned with exposing the truth, the Preacher's main
goal is to demonstrate their own brilliance, quick wittedness, and
vast stores of knowledge. While people generally see learning as
a way to better themselves, the Preacher sees learning as a means
to improve their mental dexterity and knowledge bank. Preachers
are proud of their ability to carry around disparate facts as well as
their ability to synthesize the facts that can push them to a higher
level of thought and debate. To the Preacher, an argument is both
a means and an end.

At times, Preachers get their way by convincing others of a better path, but other times they win strictly because they have worn down their opponent or colleague through mental gymnastics. Even when they win, they do not easily stop challenging the perspectives of others. It is not enough to win a point, Preachers want the other person to leave changed. One of the things that drives a Preacher to continue arguing is the search for perfection. They are not looking for what will work, or even the best that will work, but what is undeniably better than everything else. They do not agree with the concept that perfect is the enemy of good. The words "that is good enough," or "that is a fine approach," will send them reeling, regrouping, and revising their arguments. Nothing but perfection will calm them. As this is impossible, you will find the Preacher rarely satisfied.

In some aspects of their job, this will be seen as an asset. Because they are compulsive and meticulous, their work can be trusted. They work hard and are results driven. They can seem tireless, if not manic. While they may arrive at conclusions different from others, their work ethic and how they get to those conclusions will be respected, and even those who disagree with them will happily use their premises and data.

The respect colleagues have for the Preacher's ability to pull together data and facts is not appreciated by the Preacher, who can be churlish. To the Preacher, arguments and facts speak for themselves, and if the opponent of a debate looks foolish, that is as it should be. The Preacher is not concerned with the feelings of the person at the other end of the argument, only with the argument itself. Unfortunately, while they don't take things personally, it rarely occurs to them that someone else might. Because of this, it is not uncommon for pre-meetings to take place and alliances built so that colleagues come into meetings fortified and backed. If they drive away their colleagues entirely, it will be because those colleagues are either tired of debating an issue or they don't want to deal with antagonistic comments. The Preacher is the employee who goes too far. Even with their love of research and facts, Preachers can personalize things unnecessarily, alienate allies, and antagonize their competition.

Preachers have internal integrity and a strong personal set of ethics, that may or may not align with yours or the organizations. They truly seek to be the best they can be. Combined with their drive for perfection, the Preacher becomes a control freak trying to set rules and regulations around everything they do. They are their harshest critics and treat themselves worse than they treat others. In some situations, this can placate colleagues who realize the Preacher is exacting with everyone. They can become sullen if they believe they have fallen short of their goals or have disappointed their manager. This quickly turns to anger if they don't have the opportunity to lick their wounds.

TECHNIQUES TO MOTIVATE

Because of their quest for knowledge and their regular deployment of it in debates with others, Preachers are confident in their beliefs. It is easy, then, to motivate the Preacher by respecting their strong points of view and suggesting personal improvements go through this same method of debate. Use examples and build on their experiences.

Preachers love to challenge the status quo as well, so find opportunities for them to analyze current processes and working assumptions and make suggestions for changes. They will be most loyal in situations where they can readily shift ideas and attention. To have a Preacher as a sounding-board or as someone on whom to practice presentations that are expected to be spirited if not adversarial, would be motivational to both you and the Preacher.

As original thinkers who are able to build on concepts arising from their conversations with others, Preachers thrive on opportunities to be inventive, particularly with long-term problems that have vexed others. Preachers truly enjoy solving problems and knowing they have exhausted all possible pathways. They do not mind being shot down by colleagues, and you will invigorate them by putting them in charge of brainstorming sessions with people who can hold their own, but those who are not prepared to defend their positions will find the Preacher intolerant and even rude.

Preachers will be effective at getting people to think about things from new perspectives, but they will not be as successful getting people to support them individually. Although they can be charming with their confidence and sly tongue, Preachers can burn out quickly and they need to be surrounded by people who see and appreciate the details they will certainly miss. It is not to say they don't have a strong work ethic or ability to put in long hours. They do. But because of their high energy behaviors, they will need to back up and recharge regularly. Without doing so, they will lose focus and flair.

It is important to Preachers that their contributions are rewarded, and they expect to be known and acknowledged by higher-ups. They can take criticism well, and if criticisms are presented in a fair and logical manner, the Preacher will quickly course correct where needed.

PLACE ON YOUR TEAM

Preachers are independent in thought and behavior. They seek freedom to be who they are and have opportunities to explore and grow. They need to be thinking and devising. Preachers are focused on the big picture and cannot handle standard work, even though their detail-oriented perspective keeps them paying attention to the nuts and bolts of all they tend to.

Preachers don't concern themselves with niceties at the office and can end up coming across as callous. There will be people in your organization who will not want to work on teams with the Preacher, so it is best to keep the Preacher busy with highly-structured tasks, working independently, or serving in a management position where their behaviors can be chalked up to position or forgiven as a result of it. Their meetings should be kept to a minimum as they eat away at their own time as well as that of others.

Preachers will be rigid with their employees and expect you to be the same with the organization. They want people to "behave." This is rooted in their fear that they will not be able to accomplish what they need to or control the actions of others without strict rules to which they can hold people. Spontaneity and flexibility are not conditions with which they have any real comfort.

While some employees enjoy watching the Preacher argue

with others in order to see points of view working themselves out, others will find it distracting and unhelpful in advancing an agenda. Additionally, the curt nature of the Preacher can leave more sensitive people uncomfortable as they wait for a line to be crossed or feelings to be hurt. Avoid putting a Preacher in situations where the goal is consensus. Preachers should be in positions where they are actively thinking, analyzing, and communicating their points. At higher levels, they are effective lawyers, labor leaders, research scientists, start-up executives, and turn-around agents. In lower positions, they are adept at gate-keeping, collections, and security.

EXAMPLES OF PREACHERS

Ayn Rand

Writer; philosopher; political activist

Jed Rakoff

Attorney; adjunct professor of law, Columbia University; authority on securities law; US Attorney; United States District Judge

Reshma Saujani

Attorney; founder, Girls Who Code; candidate, U.S. House of Representatives; advocate for gender equality

THE FABRICATOR

"I have blueprints for an ark, but I can't tell you where I got them."

PROFILE

The Fabricator is an Accomplice who is self-assured and idealistic. They truly like people and the connections they make are often at an emotional level that both parties find particularly fulfilling. Even at work, Fabricators are able to connect with others in a meaningful way that seems authentic. This is in large part because they can read people and pick up on nuances that others might miss. They see people as they are and rarely seek to change them. Because they take the time to understand both people and situations, Fabricators have an uncanny ability to predict the consequences of events. They almost appear psychic when, in fact, they are just keen observers who like to put puzzle pieces together.

While they seek to have genuine relationships with others, the Fabricator's energy—which tends to either be charismatic or flighty–can unnerve some colleagues and keep them at bay. Their demeanor, and even their clothes, can seem non-traditional and perhaps even off-putting. Luckily the Fabricator is a deft communicator, who knows how to push the right buttons for each individual, whether they seek to inspire or discourage. Fabricators have to be careful that they do not come across as too slick and self-serving. They generally aren't, but others can be suspicious of charismatic people who speak well and connect with them. The more mature Fabricator understands this and patiently imparts knowledge and guides from the side.

Fabricators are free spirits who are hungry for new experiences. This does not mean they want constant excitement. Fabricators are content to relax and find enjoyment in even the smallest of things and simplest of activities. They are just eager to learn, grow, and bring others along. They are not always forthcoming, however. They maintain power and mystique by having answers but not sharing how they got them. Fabricators ensnare others with their charm and willingness to share advice and guidance, but they keep a wall around them. Their strong personality may be a mechanism to exclude others.

Fabricators are consummate observers who try to take in every sight, sound, and smell in an attempt to further stimulate their imaginations and connect them to current situations. Their enthusiasm to share their experiences captivates others and increases the intimacy others will feel. This enables them to be valuable creatives at work as well as advocates for what they have developed, whether ideas, products, or processes.

They are sensitive and express this in their emotions whether they are sharing how they feel or empathizing with another. This is one of the reasons so many people look up to them. They are gregarious, but still unassuming. They also take the time to listen and get to know the other. They can even match their own energy to their immediate colleagues, making them even more relatable and appealing. Fabricators can come into a room like gang-busters, but if they sense the mood of the room is more relaxed and solemn, they calm themselves, thereby building trust. Fabricators are consummate shape shifters.

Fabricators are good employees who love to create and build. But whether they are pitching their own creation or that of another, they are talented and cunning campaigners. Others easily understand the points they make and happily follow. The Fabricator is intriguing and, therefore, great at garnering attention. Because they only attempt to get others to believe them when they feel their cause is worthy, they are effective in convincing others to go their way. This confidence and search for what is right also means the Fabricator can get lost in their own circular thinking. As a result, they can end up down a path of obsessiveness.

TECHNIQUES TO MOTIVATE

The Fabricator is an optimistic dreamer who seeks to find a deeper meaning in life through observation and connection to others. Because Fabricators are naturally curious as well as spiritual, they try to understand everything by asking, "Why does this matter?" and, "How is everything connected?" This includes connecting people and helping everyone be their best at work. This also makes the Fabricator popular, which in turn inspires them to do more good for more people. The best way to motivate them is to tap into their ability to pull a crowd together around a single issue, event, or goal.

While Fabricators are people-pleasers at heart, they are not focused simply on being liked. They want to make a difference in the lives of others. Fabricators can be quite compassionate and do not have any difficulty focusing in on the needs of others. To motivate a Fabricator, give them opportunities to cut a new path and inspire others with their originality. Give them a team to rally and help them with mundane work they will find difficult to complete. If they are micromanaged, they will falter, and their followers will likewise lose energy and focus. If you find the Fabricator faltering, help them step back to see long-term implications and allow them the opportunity to argue with you to help find their way. Fabricators are intrinsically motivated and tend to think all people are that way. They engage with colleagues based on that assumption, and they don't like, or even understand, a company that bases motivation on any type of conditioning behavior, whether it is reward or punishment.

It is in your best interest to tap into the extrovert and socializing nature of the Fabricator. They like to be the center of attention, not because it feeds their ego, but because it gives them the opportunity to make more human connections. Human connections fuel their thought processes and creativity and make them feel vital and needed.

PLACE ON YOUR TEAM

Fabricators care about the well-being of others, but they do not put others ahead of themselves. They are independent and fiercely protect their own needs and interests. So, while their intensity and affable nature influences others to follow them, they generally don't like to be in leadership positions that require self-sacrifice, a loss of freedom to be unique and innovative, or responsibility to repetitive administrative tasks. Fabricators also don't like to keep their emotions tamped down the way a leader must. Their tendencies to personalize and emotionalize situations can be detrimental at work. Fabricators who are more junior employees will need to be coached away from this while Fabricators who are more senior will need to work in small teams from which they can go off to decompress and even pout.

There is nothing that you could ask of a Fabricator that would take them out of their comfort zone when it comes to confidence in their own talents and ability to compensate for gaps by using the skills of others. Their natural inquisitiveness enables them to easily move from one challenge to the next, one job to another, and from one physical location to a different place altogether. When they get frustrated or overwhelmed, it generally is at themselves and their inability to stop their inquiry and experimenting and bring things to a conclusion.

Fabricators are proficient communicators. They naturally gravitate to jobs where they can combine their vast interests and interact with many people. They are good at and enjoy juggling a multitude of tasks. They particularly like being with similar people who seek fun and excitement in the context of authentic relationships. Because they are so good with people, Fabricators work well in liaison positions. They can read a room and, therefore, prepare it for you or vice versa. They are adept public relations representatives, customer service agents, corporate psychologists, salespeople, executive assistants, restructuring staff, and lobbyists. Their work relationships often spill into friendships that last a long time.

EXAMPLES OF FABRICATORS

Diana Princess of Wales

Philanthropist; patron; humanitarian

Juliana Rotich

Information technology professional; developer of crowdsourcing tools; trustee, Bankinter Foundation for Entrepreneurship and Innovation

Harriet Beecher Stowe

Abolitionist; author; co-founder, University of Hartford

THE DEVISER

"There will be a flood. I have connections, and I can save you…

for the right price."

PROFILE

The Deviser is an Accomplice who is distinguished and confident, if not arrogant. They will thrust themselves into the center of attention where they can feel in control of their message and the responses of other people. Fortunately for them, Devisers know how to keep this attention through wit, insight, and high energy. Even those who suspect the Deviser might have an agenda find themselves entranced. Devisers can effectively work a room and delight others with their charm and ready quips, and they quickly will pivot if they are not receiving the intended reaction. For the Devisers, truth is not essential; it is secondary to persuasion, as the end justifies the means.

Devisers love to regale others with stories of their adventures and exploits. They are goal oriented, so whether they are bragging about a contract they landed or a mountain they climbed, Devisers can garner attention via their successes. The paradox surrounding Devisers is that they are relatively cold and detached when not in the spotlight, so their popularity is more superficial than people might realize. Colleagues will think they know Devisers more than they do and believe they are closer to them than they really are. This benefits the Deviser as people will follow, but they will not have to divulge more than they want or need.

Devisers like to keep busy and live in the here and now. When you find an urgent need, the Deviser is likely to have capacity. You can turn to them when you need unexpected help or an inventive approach from someone with a knack for manipulation. When the Deviser chooses to engage people, it is to advance particular objectives. To be helpful, they need to understand the greater plan and what you hope to accomplish. Their cooperation needs to have a purpose and a personal benefit to them.

Devisers keep themselves in the know and parlay their knowledge into connections and deals. They are very transactional in nature, and because they are not particularly trusting of others, they prefer to manage their relationships and activities through formal agreements or at least a set of rules. Devisers are equally comfortable working collaboratively or alone, but when they are not the highlight of the conversation or activity, their demeanor can be arrogant and off-putting. Because Devisers can be intimidating, many colleagues will not find them approachable. It takes time and personal interactions for people to warm up to Devisers and vice versa.

Devisers are loud and proud. They spend much of their energy convincing others of their great accomplishments and ambitious goals. This is easily done because they tend to be successful. They always are thinking, plotting, and deploying others, and if necessary, Devisers get things done through sheer will and strength of character. Given enough time, colleagues will see sufficient achievement from the Deviser that the wake left behind them ultimately will be forgiven, and detractors will become confederates. Besides, their "ready, fire, aim" mentality has given Devisers plenty of opportunities to assess situations, learn facts quickly, make immediate decisions, and clean-up messes, skills that can be appreciated by colleagues and especially supervisors.

Devisers are hopeful types who most fear not mattering. That is what is behind their need for attention. They want to feel valuable to the team, and while they primarily are goal-oriented at any cost, they truly seek to push themselves and others to be the best. When something is high stakes or mission-focused, Devisers can become crusaders. When this is the case, they will spin a yarn to bolster support. To them, exaggerating the situation and embellishing the facts is a ready strategy for leading a mission.

TECHNIQUES TO MOTIVATE

Devisers are perceptive and prefer to learn from experience, so you will get more out of them by providing hands-on experience in the tactics you will need them to employ. Even if they are seasoned workers, they will continue to learn and mature as long as they have opportunities to make mistakes and course correct. If their attention can be concentrated where you want, Devisers can effectively add excitement that will help engage others. Put them where you want boundaries to be pushed.

Devisers live in the moment, so it is best to keep them focused on immediate needs and busy with specific tactics and responsibilities. Be precise and tell them what you need, why, and when. Having well-documented milestones with due dates will serve you and the Deviser well. Be clear with them, and they will be clear back. This includes making sure they understand what is not for public consumption. They are not particularly discreet, so you will need to let them know directly what to keep secretive. They are assertive and self-assured and will unabashedly run toward the goal, leaving others bruised and bewildered along the way. Because they are so focused on the here and now, they are incentivized by recognition of what they have accomplished, even if it is a simple "nice job."

When it is time to have a more critical conversation with the Deviser, it is essential that you are oriented toward the practical and provide the Deviser with examples. Make sure that you are correct in your assessment as the Deviser will challenge you. Also make sure you focus on your belief in an improved future. The Deviser will respond well and quickly to "help me help you." If they trust they can improve their own situation while bringing life to others, they will eagerly take your suggestions. Likewise, if they see an ability to maintain their boundary-pushing bold persona, they will accept practical constraints and limitations.

PLACE ON YOUR TEAM

The Deviser is a risk-taker who continuously looks for opportunities to stimulate their own minds and emotions. They enjoy taking chances because it gives them an opportunity to solve problems quickly and with some stakes involved. In the right positions, where you are open to a level of uncertainty and exposure, they can provide ingenuity. Similarly, they are strong in positions where it is their job to assess the risks others are taking and suggest proper mitigation or redirection.

The Deviser requires regular check-ins, and at times direct supervision, because their penchant for crossing the line includes your organization's rules and regulations. They don't like to be told what to do, or that they are not allowed to do something, by people who are not their direct supervisors or do not, in their minds, have the intellectual or moral authority to give them orders. Those are fighting words. This makes it difficult to find the right place on your team for them. Devisers are not skilled at allowing for, or even caring about, unintended consequences, so make sure to surround them with people who are. If they are in managerial positions, they probably have figured this out themselves and delegate people to tend to repercussions. Because their minds are always thinking about immediate tactical needs, they are prone to miss the big picture or jump from one big picture to another. This is fine if they are geniuses, but for regular people this can be problematic. When Devisers are not successful, they can become deceitful to ensure the right appearance. Still, the Deviser is a driver who can help stimulate a team and give them someone to rally around.

Devisers can be bullshit artists, but they think rationally and logically, so they are effective in positions where you need controlled chaos and rapid change. They are natural experimenters who like to put ideas and products together in unique ways with an eye to quick responsiveness. They will meet due dates, and even be aggressive in helping to set them. Because of their propensity for maneuvering around others, they can quickly pick up on the subtleties others may not notice, whether it be a facial expression, body language, or a change in behavior. They can be helpful reading a room. They are effectual directors of innovation, research and design managers, spin-off entrepreneurs, salespeople, activists, and organizers.

EXAMPLES OF DEVISERS

Mahatma Gandhi

Attorney; anti-colonial nationalist; political ethicist; civil rights activist and nonviolent resister.

Elon Musk

Engineer; founder PayPal; CEO, Tesla; founder and CEO, SpaceX; co-founder, SolarCity

Greta Thunberg

Environmental activist; author

THE USER

"There will be a flood, and someone needs to figure
something out."

PROFILE

The User is an Accomplice with a bold and engaging personality
that's generally fun and friendly. This appeals to their colleagues'
need for diversions, entertainment, and escape. Users know people
want to spend time with them, which is how they seduce them
into doing things or joining activities—which supports avoiding
something they find unappealing or unrewarding. Users gain the
attention of others with down-right showmanship, but they entice
them to participate in their antics with passion, pleasure, and
sensuality. Their goal is not to control others in order to achieve
a particular end but, rather, to possess them through intrigue and
mystery. Ideally, Users would like to be admired. They don't seek
to manipulate people as much as to develop a co-dependent relationship whereby they have a fan and fellow conspirator.

The User is a seeker of fun and wants relationships with people who will be captivated and distracted by them. Users are people others truly enjoy being with and the subsequent socializing will cause Users to neglect duties at-hand and not worry about the consequences. Their optimistic spirit keeps them believing that things will work out for them, and often it does because their likeability masks the fact they are taking advantage of people or situations. Their belief that things will work out for them is not always proven true, however, and when the User is reprimanded or fired, they will see the silver lining and turn the event into a new opportunity.

The User connects through intimacy and generosity. They will develop a closeness with others and share secrets, whether they are plans for the future or stories from the past. They will be benevolent with time, money, flattery, and hospitality. However, there are strings attached. The User keeps score and will be sure that the tally is in their favor. If the User helps you or one of your employees on a project, you can be sure that a request on behalf of the User is on the way. The User will scarcely care if that favor is bigger than what was received or requested at an inconvenient time.

Their self-reliance and intellect are admired and appreciated because Users are independent, self-assured, and domineering in a way that gives security to many people. Users are naturally spontaneous, and their air of confidence during such actions can cause others to overestimate how smart and brave they are. Because their careers are sprinkled with success, whether fully earned or not, Users often are given the benefit of the doubt. They also are extremely adept at jumping on the right team or signing the right report to ensure they are attached to success. Users have trouble staying on task, in large part, because they hope their procrastination will result in someone else just doing the work while they get back to being enchanting and admired.

The User is able to gain the trust of others, but they are not quick to trust. They naturally are suspicious of other people, which is one of the reasons they spend so much time trying to razzle dazzle. They are, for the most part, conflict averse so they will avoid trouble–such as hanging around when a deadline has been missed–and unnecessary intimacy–such as sharing information with colleagues beyond what is needed to get the job done.

Users are able to be what people need or want to see. Whether male or female, the User will also rely on physical appearance and sex appeal to garner support and gain influence. Much of this is an attempt to keep things superficial. Users do not like conflict.

TECHNIQUES TO MOTIVATE

Users are emotional, and they easily get carried away by whatever fun or interesting activity is in front of them. They like a work environment that is stimulating, ever-changing, and even turbid. If they can step in and offer a solution, or at least advice, they are thrilled with the attention. If they can do this in an informal setting where they can use impromptu humor, they can command attention that is mutually fulfilling.

The User needs and seeks attention and, since they are always keeping score, they need to know how they are doing relative to specific goals and particular people. Users will overshoot, so help them make sure their goals are realistic and provide them with appropriate rationale to help keep them engaged. Because their colleagues often find them captivating, make sure to strategically tap into their influencer powers. Because of their knowledge of people and fun-loving personalities, Users are able to attract their own loyal followings. Take advantage of this opportunity because, if you can gain their loyalty, Users can help you spread your message.

It is not easy to corral the User and get them to improve performance. One way is to spend enough time with them that they feel valued as you coach them. Stress the importance of your relationship with them and assure them that they have not lost your fealty. The best way to motivate a User, however, is to keep them on track by tapping into their vitality and ingenuity. If you can do this while guiding them to manipulate a vendor or customer through guile and conjuring, you will activate their sweet spot.

Users are more practical than you might suspect given their gregarious personas. While truth might be relative to them, their decisions, particularly about their own futures, will be rooted in a realistic sense of what they are and are not capable of accomplishing. Their manner may be garish, but their processes and tactics will be functional and feasible.

PLACE ON YOUR TEAM

Users truly can be plopped in where you need them. They don't really have comfort zones, so you can deploy them in situations and with duties that are new to them, and they won't make a fuss. They likely will even find it exciting as the newness will quash any boredom and, of course, new coworkers mean new audience members.

Users enjoy trying new and interesting things and can ignite a fire in others. When there is something new happening—a move, product release, marketing campaign or the like–the User can spark interest and rally the troops. You must keep in mind, though, that they can lose interest in things quickly and, when this occurs, they can become inattentive or careless. Wherever and whenever you use them, have contingencies in place. The User is not going to be paying attention to long-term consequences so you must.

It is better to focus them on strategies rather than tactics and to keep them away from detailed work. Because they have a habit of using others, and because they don't have any follow-through, they have not developed any expertise. They truly are masters of none, and they will lean heavily on others to do their work. But they are creative, and they enjoy things that are non-conventional, so are particularly gifted at learning new things and then being placed in a position to teach others. They enjoy both the experimenting and the demonstrating.

Users are highly sensual, meaning they thrive where their senses are being used; i.e., places that are noisy, colorful, or fragrant. Careers involving travel, cooking, the arts, or other ways to activate the senses will bring out the best in the User. Aesthetics matter to them. They have an innate ability to recognize both quality and worth, so they are natural entertainers, product developers, salespeople, and marketers. Their keen interest in showing off would make them good brand marketers as well and their beguiling personalities lend themselves well to positions such as spokespeople and convention booth staff.

EXAMPLES OF USERS

Nancy Wake

Nurse; journalist; spy

Emeril Lagasse

Chef; television personality; author; restaurateur; philanthropist

Jennifer Lopez

Dancer; actor; producer; clothing designer; activist

ADVERSARIES

THE BLAMER

"It's going to flood, and no one has bothered to

build an ark."

PROFILE

The Blamer is an Adversary who prefers to be left alone. This is one of the reasons they point the finger quickly at others. The Blamer has a need to be right, but they also seek to be out of sight and out of mind. When the going gets tough, the Blamer retreats. They can quash their own fear by passing accountability and consequences on to someone else. They are masters at keeping eyes off of themselves just in case things go sideways.

Blamers are guided by their principles and want to be judged according to them as well. This results in them being slow to apologize or admit they are wrong. Part of this is plain stubbornness, part is apprehension at taking responsibility and getting into trouble. But, mostly, their resistance to admitting they are wrong is that they just don't see it. The principles that guide Blamers are often different from those that guide their colleagues. Their morality is more fluid and rooted in selfishness.

They are motivated by fear which causes them to avoid obligations, and they are quick to incriminate others, which allows them to take some risk. This combination makes it difficult to predict where the Blamer may or may not step up and take authority. Blamers also can end up in personal stalemates and be downright careless about their own duties.

Blamers are quiet introverts who often are unnoticed by those with whom they do not interact. They take things personally and suffer silently, so those who do work with them may see them as lost souls or cowards. They are indeed aloof, but surprisingly, they seek harmony. Often this is accomplished by getting others to take on challenges that might result in mistakes and missteps. The Blamer appears to be collaborative in communicating goals and activities that others can take on, however the underlying motive is to put someone else in place to take responsibility when things go south. Harmony is quickly lost among those who know the Blamer well. The Blamer may be quiet and conflict averse, but those around them won't always be. Blamers will bring out the resentment and anger of those who have been thrown under the bus by the Blamer or left holding the bag. Blamers already take things too personally, so any criticism is often unbearable, causing them to disengage from colleagues and fuel mistrust.

They are pessimistic and see problems far sooner than they see anything positive. Blamers are nervous, doubtful people. If they are going to believe something, they are going to have to see it themselves. When they do believe or support something, they can become outright fanatics. They get behind a cause or project only if it ultimately serves their own interests. What they can't get behind is something that brings about too much change. They will take a conservative approach and resist new ideas they deem untested or unconventional.

Similar to the way they repress the truth—especially when it makes them look bad—Blamers are able to repress their own feelings. They are detached from what is happening around them and don't consider the long-term consequences. They just want to look good without taking responsibility for successes or failures. No one minds that Blamers don't take credit for a job well done, but they are widely resented for their ability to quickly disavow a person or situation where something has gone wrong.

Like most people, the Blamer is trying to find their place in the world, but they are not having success. They are lost searchers. Their searching will cause them to be militant followers of leaders who are brash and coercive. Blamers are capable of idolizing such people, and when they do, they will not hesitate to turn over their will and reconstruct their principles accordingly.

TECHNIQUES TO MOTIVATE

Blamers care about their careers, and they respond to positive feedback. They seek structure in the world and in the workplace through obedience—theirs and their colleagues'. This can prompt them to become proactive in seeking out something meaningful to do. Their approach will be cautious, and in the early stages of a project or opportunity, they will appear sensitive and responsive. A leader can motivate them by building on those attributes, guiding their sensitivity to things that matter to the Blamer and being responsive in a way that validates.

Since Blamers are motivated by envy, you can get some mileage from pointing out the successes of others. Blamers tend to overwork themselves, and they will do what they can to meet deadlines and your approval. If they are overworking themselves to the point of exhaustion, or if envy is getting the better of them, you can refocus the Blamer by working on a long-term plan and by brainstorming with them different ways to get there.

Blamers take tradition seriously and are willing to do things because "that is the way they have always been done." This philosophy also extends to history in general. If something is grounded in tradition or has survived the test of time, the Blamer is going to be more comfortable with it. This all means, in part, that Blamers do not like change. You will best motivate them by keeping them in the same position, in the same department, for years. This also is a good way for you to keep an eye on them.

Blamers need to be watched, because they are not team players and do not cooperate for the greater good. Although they generally are polite, and often can be friendly, they will not hesitate to throw someone under the bus, which means that few people will work with them. This lack of buy-in from colleagues leaves them isolated, with little information, and a fair amount of frustration, if not anger.

They do not grow from criticism, so it is best to present to Blamers with facts about their performance which are tied to metrics that they can digest on their own.

PLACE ON YOUR TEAM

Blamers generally are detached from others and lack empathy, which is why it's so easy for them to disparage others. They are antagonistic and talk in circles if things are not going their way, so they are best left to solo work where their responsibility cannot be questioned and their aloofness does not affect others. If you put them under the radar, Blamers can be more effective.

They are not your best employees and will need coaching and supervision. It is good to document their missteps as soon as they are observed so you have a record on which to fire them when that time comes, and it likely will. Blamers are hard employees to coach out or prompt to resign as they truly are gifted at arguing how it really was somebody else's fault. While they are seen as emotionless, that can change if they feel insecure or cannot avoid the blame that should reside with them. Their propensity to blame can quickly shift to ridicule and bullying if they feel cornered.

Blamers can be effective managers if they are smart and experienced but, in large part, their seeming effectiveness simply is the result of someone else taking the blame for their mistakes or miscalculations. Their mistakes can go unnoticed through their effective shift of attention and responsibility. If they are managing a team, it could take time for them to be held accountable as they point the finger at their own team. If they are inexperienced and, therefore, more inclined to fail, the scapegoating will not matter as they will not be able to course-correct and will not have a team supporting them as they seek to. If you find you need to keep a

Blamer because problems have not been adequately documented and the time is not right to fire them, or because the Blamer has a particular skill set you need at the moment, it is best to treat them as sole contributors. This will enable you to draw a straight line from their work to consequences. It also will help keep chaos to a minimum so you won't have to spend time untangling responsibilities or fallout. Try to use their experience or expertise in positions such as analysists, researchers, or consultants.

THE DICTATOR

"I told you it was going to rain, don't listen to anyone else from now on. I alone will save us when the flood comes."

PROFILE

The Dictator is an Adversary who is a self-taught leader with some natural tendencies to garner followers. The Dictator is an arrogant and stubborn know-it-all. Occasionally right and routinely annoying, their charisma sits well on only a few. This is because their quest for authority and control will cause them to run roughshod over others. Their personalities often are overwhelming because their energy is focused, their demeanor domineering, and their ability to manage the emotions of others almost non-existent. Dictators do not care how people feel and see it as a weakness when others do.

Obsessed with victory, the Dictator will seek to win at any cost. They enjoy challenges because they believe they will, given enough time and resources, prevail. They are artful at putting together a strong team and then commanding it. And, while they can be cold and ruthless, they still will have followers because people want to be on the winning team or find comfort in the rules and structure the Dictator puts in place. The Dictator cannot personally abide rules and structure, but they are paramount when it comes to controlling others. Through the combination of their hyperbole, seeming quest for ideals, and formal hierarchy, Dictators present a façade of superiority and paramountcy.

The Dictator is optimistic in the sense of believing what they believe and then being proud simply of the belief: "I think it, therefore it is true." Whether it is good news or bad news, they will point out that they had the news ahead of time. Then they will suggest that they have access to information no one else has or that the opposition's information simply should not be trusted. Dictator's use information to show their power and influence. This works on many people who don't have access to the same knowledge, are easily influenced, or just want to be in proximity to power. The Dictator will not have trouble finding people to fall under their spell.

The Dictator can read and deploy people effectively, but they might have trouble keeping peers on the team. The Dictator loves taking credit for things which will discourage those who also seek praise or the opportunity to rise. Dictators also like to show-off, primarily with things that signify exclusivity or luxury. Their more down-to-earth colleagues will be turned off by this and may even try to mitigate the Dictator's power. If the Dictator finds such a threat to authority, or their path to it, they will stop at nothing to defeat or quash their detractors, stooping even to lies, false flags, and gas-lighting.

Their self-assuredness causes Dictators to look down on other people and be disdainful of the ideas of others. They are highly judgmental. They will discard ideas that are not on track with their goals and demean ideas that seem rooted in gut feelings or doing something based on the emotional well-being of others. This is also the case if they believe the ideas of others will not ultimately support their quest for power.

Because Dictators are smart and may arrive at conclusions faster than many, they will develop goals and strategies before even considering alternative paths. This will cause others to dislike and distrust them even before they have a chance to demonstrate their abrasive personalities. This dislike is exacerbated because the Dictator is unkind. They are intolerant of differences, unforgiving of mistakes, scornful of the less intelligent, and impatient with most people and situations. Even when someone is smarter and harder working than they are, the Dictator is not likely to see it or believe it. Their outrageous confidence is largely a result of overestimating their own prowess and underestimating that of others.

TECHNIQUES TO MOTIVATE

Dictators may be disciplined and hardworking only because they hope their efforts will clear a path to absolute power. They are clearly focused on the goal to one day being in charge, and they are Machiavellian in their approach. They are interested in control, not actual knowledge or accurate facts, so they easily justify saying and doing almost anything to advance themselves. They are fine with making things up as they go. Their approach will be strategic, if not forthright. They are motivated by the opportunity to use their communication skills to get others to clear their path or fall for their rhetoric.

Dictators seek to connect with others through control and manipulation. The Dictator does not live by the thinking of others. They forge their own trail and are proud to do so. This is how they see and sell themselves. Provide the Dictator with opportunities to be right but, more importantly, provide them with scenarios where logic is valued. The Dictator takes pride in courage, so you can motivate them by putting them in high-risk scenarios or where bombastic oratory is confused for strength.

Tenacity is the strongest asset of the Dictator and the characteristic that provides the foundation for all other personality traits. They will plow forward where others would be filled with self-doubt or at least cautionary questioning. Dictators have the ability to push others into action as well, so by giving them a team, you will motivate them and see results. They are astute at seeing and using the talents of others. However, the Dictator will be rude, and can be mean, to those who don't live up to their standards. Dictators are dogmatic, so the only guarantee that your goals, or the organization's goals, will remain front and center is if they are part and parcel with the tenets the Dictator is driving. The Dictator always will put their needs first. So, while they will most likely be successful at reaching their goals, there probably will be figurative dead bodies along the way. Keeping a Dictator on your payroll will mean you have to continuously assess the risk-benefit.

PLACE ON YOUR TEAM

The Dictator is on a mission to get to the top, so they job hop to ensure they are in positions of power and influence that also act as stepping stones. Dictators know how to use their charm to keep people distracted, and they also know how to wield knowledge to keep people at arm's length. This means that, even if you recognize the Dictator in your midst, you probably don't know your Dictator as well as you think. Their tenure with you likely has been short as well, leaving little of a track record. Be cautious with how much authority and latitude you give to them.

You can best use the Dictator when you need to change the mind of skeptics who have yet to form an opinion of the Dictator, or when you need to have facts delivered in an authoritarian, coercive manner. Logical decision-making will guide the Dictator, and their combative nature will keep them fighting for what they, and presumably you, believe. It is imperative, therefore, that you get the Dictator on your side before deploying them to do anything. Dictators are good in your legal or government affairs departments, as negotiators, or as handlers—if you trust them enough to share information and power.

The Dictator counts on being right, so they will be detail- and process-oriented. If that fails, the Dictator will use their vast stores of knowledge to just make something up that is bound to have some truth in it, or so they think. The Dictator is relentless and vicious, so they will fight until they have achieved what they set out to. Their own behaviors can seem highly structured, but they do not thrive in highly-structured environments. They need the freedom to rise above rules and laws or create new ones to fit their agenda. They do not care about feelings—theirs or others. This has its benefits if you are using them to combat enemies, but in an organization that is not involved in corporate espionage, legal battles, or toe-to-toe skirmishes with competitors or regulators, this kind of antagonism will be turned inward toward you or other employees. It's best not to keep this personality around.

THE POSER

"It's going to rain; I'll be in my office working. You all should
build the ark I invented."

PROFILE

The Poser is an Adversary who may be the most difficult employee
to identify. Posers are nimble opportunists who can take on
whatever personality traits or dispositions necessary to accomplish
their goals. They can fly under the radar, but more nefariously,
they operate as masqueraders who endeavor to appear to be loyal,
competent, hardworking, or all three. Posers are self-centered. Their
goals differ—some want power, some money, some acclaim—but
what they have in common is the ability to become what you or
your company need. They are con-artists and liars who put all of
their energy into their deception in hopes of not having to really
earn credentials or tend to actual tasks.

To be effective tricksters, Posers are friendly and successful at
bringing people together to form a community that they can blend

into. For the most part, their way of being accepted and trusted is through the credibility that comes with being one of the gang. If they are aloof, it is for the sole purpose of being off-putting enough to dissuade people from digging into who they really are and how they really spend their time. They don't want people to become aware of their agendas or career paths. Their ultimate goal is merely to keep their jobs, something they are not particularly good at because they never fully connect to people or company missions, and they are too quick to lie and pretend to be someone they are not. Their lies catch up to them. In their perfect world, Posers would have secure jobs, maybe even tenured or union jobs and the corresponding security without having to make an effort, but short of that, they will do what they can to appear more competent and effective than they are. They want security, so Posers won't quit a position unless their behavior is finally uncovered.

Because they are faking so much in their own lives, Posers generally project their characteristics on others and become quickly suspicious of others. They assume there is an element to everyone that is not as it seems, and they spend too much time looking for it or worrying about it. They are skilled at maintaining a low profile, so regardless of their own fears of discovery and suspicions of other people, they will be cooperative and collaborative while taking care not to go the extra mile. Ironically, this does not mean that they are detached from success or reward.

One of the most unexpected and interesting things about the Poser is that they can come to care about results and their image. Unfortunately, because they are pretending to be more than they are, they have to take credit for more than they have done. They will join teams, make other people take risks, and then stand proud when compliments and accolades follow. Similarly, they neurotically concern themselves with social status and appearing to have more than they do. They will present themselves as having proper social graces and protocol and as being both gracious and polished, but they will possess items they cannot afford and spend money they do not have in order to impress people who do not care and may not even notice.

Posers are rudderless and do not have core beliefs on which to depend for direction, they will, however, rely on the needs of other people for order and customs. They are observant of the behaviors around them, but they prefer to keep the focus on them and will quickly use humor to both connect with others and pull attention back to themselves. They enjoy playing the jester. When they have goals and direction, they likely will be based on keeping their reputation, ensuring their agenda is followed, or meeting essential requirements to keep their job. In such cases, they are able to bide their time and be patient.

TECHNIQUES TO MOTIVATE

While Posers are adroit shapeshifters, seeking to be all things to all people, they are surprisingly inflexible. Because they cannot risk being uncovered as less than what they portray, they quickly dismiss the concepts and plans of others if they cannot keep control of all moving parts. They become stressed out to the level of making a scene if they are unable to control a situation.

Posers are highly judgmental of other people, especially in regard to rank and status. They don't want others at their own perceived level and seem to look down upon their peers as a result. They like to keep people on edge and insecure and they will quickly discredit others' work, not to elevate their own, but just for the game. They often conduct this behavior in passive-aggressive ways so that they don't lose any support from the community they have created. You can motivate them by complimenting them regularly and keeping them focused on themselves and how they are perceived. Combine this with a focus on actual milestones, and you might be able to get meaningful work out of them.

It is difficult for Posers to relax, and they often are viewed as manic. Their short fuses and quick mood changes can create a volatile environment. They may seem reflective, but they only appear so to manipulate the situation, not to improve. They live in the moment. If you can give them short-term goals or at least regular and frequent milestones, they will see their success and, thereby, develop some self-worth that you can use for motivating them.

Posers are adept at using energy wisely, even if you find some of the energy to be negative or negatively spent. This means they can be fast and efficient and reliable for short-term goals. Where they have particular staying power is around their own ambitions, so if you can catch that wave, you will be most effective with them.

PLACE ON YOUR TEAM

Posers hate authority, and this attitude will extend to those in positions of authority. Any appearance that the Poser is respecting you or your position is sycophantic. They will appear to acquiesce to your desires and dictates, but they will pursue their own agenda. They are experts at the smile and nod. So, if you find a need to have a Poser on your team, make sure that their agenda aligns with yours or vice versa. It also is best to approach them from a posture of democracy and consensus. Even if both of you know that you have the final say, their sensibilities and posturing will respond favorable to the gesture. Posers also distrust those they see as blindly following rules, so to build their own teams, they rely on personality and mission rather than hierarchy and authority.

Posers are carpetbaggers and tricksters. Their made-up persona goes deeper than bravado. Their resume is likely a series of made-up positions, titles, or responsibilities—or all of the above. You will not be able to trust them, but if you are in need of corporate espionage or any sort of duplicity, you may find a use for them. Posers usually are not a good fit in any organization because their lack of veracity is pathological, so when they do seem to be working out, it could be that you are missing signs or just being conned. If you are adept at seeing through lies, or have enough safety mechanisms in place, you could use Posers to execute short-term tactics. Otherwise, they are going to be in their offices looking busy and likely demoralizing the people on your team who really are working.

They best way to get a Poser out the door is to professionally make their shortcomings public by focusing on metrics and milestones not being met. Their concern with social status will have them quitting before you have time to fire them.

THE AGITATOR

"There will be a flood, and we're all going to die."

PROFILE

The Agitator is an Adversary whose existence and posturing in your organization is no secret. They cause eye rolls and sighs when they add their opinions and sometimes just by entering a room. They frustrate and anger their colleagues because that is their intent, though it is rarely everyone at one time. They are seen as an outlaw, the bad boy (or girl). Don't assume, however, that this reputation will take care of itself when colleagues shun them or shy away. Many Agitators become popular, and their colleagues will use them to get their own unpopular messages across. The Agitator is not afraid of going out on a limb, and they appreciate being viewed as a rebel when something unpopular needs to be said or done. Their relationships with colleagues can be symbiotic in a way that threatens authority when their behavior seeks to incite, or results in, rabble-rousing.

The Agitator's ability to successfully get under the skin of others is rooted in their skills for observing what gets a rise out of others and their tendency to see worst case scenarios. They enjoy poking the rattle snake because they think someone needs to, and they are recalcitrant when they have staked out their position. Yet, their ability to be motivating and develop a resonating rhetoric should not be underestimated. To more junior staff—or to all staff if you do not have strong communication within your company during times of upheaval—Agitators can sound as if they alone have found the answer or they alone care what is happening. They like escalating things and creating conflict for the sheer fun of it. One of the ways they escalate is by being competitive, often when unnecessary or even inappropriate.

They are fiercely private and few will know them well. They are not forthcoming about their personal lives, activities, or motivations. They shut down when they feel misunderstood, unappreciated, or if they made a mistake that has gotten attention. They don't recognize personal boundaries and think nothing of getting into the business of others and sharing theirs. Because they are overly competitive, this inability to recognize boundaries comes across as a strategy to learn the weaknesses and vulnerabilities of others. The Agitator is not disciplined enough to start on that course, but once they have information on someone else, they will use it to their competitive advantage including overt manipulation. They often become outcasts within the informal culture.

Agitators are misguided souls who suffer from low self-esteem and strive to find ways to build themselves up or at least feel alive. This can manifest as contrariness. They argue, not to come to a different conclusion or to compromise with the ideas of others, but rather out of spite. They seek to tear others down to build themselves up. This is their path to making themselves relevant. This makes them feel relevant. This relevancy feeds their ego. They do not need to have people see what they have accomplished or even be appreciative of it. So, while they are comfortable being the "yeah, but" person in the room, they are far more satisfied by throwing tactical bombs and psychological grenades. They stir things up from a distance—often anonymously–and make sure they are well out of the way of shrapnel. Their need to matter and their need to muddle makes it nearly impossible to predict their behavior

They are spirited and compelling. When they end up leading a revolution or developing a cult following, they do so reluctantly as they seek fundamental change, not popularity. The exception would be if they were protesting something that requires a critical mass and they were imperative to that. They dislike commitments and continuously will be looking for other opportunities as they make soft or quasi-promises. They need to be critical to the cause. When they are not, they quickly move on.

TECHNIQUES TO MOTIVATE

Agitators engage in risky behaviors in their personal lives as well as at work because they thrive on excitement and negative attention. But even positive attention will get you some mileage from them. Think of them like a teenager. When an Agitator is pointing out problems, especially while visibly stressed out themselves, you and your managers should not stoop to arguing. It is important to not fuel the volatile energy of the Agitator. Instead, build on the Agitator's concerns or redirect them. If the Agitator says the floods are going to kill everyone, then focus on what should be done until the floods arrive. Whatever your organization's main issues, use the Agitator to keep you on your toes. They always will see the worst in any situation. Consider them as the enemy who tests your mettle. Let them dig up the negatives about what you are doing before your competitors or the press can. Motivate them by allowing them some room to push back on plans or policies, since this benefits you, and their days are numbered. Just control the context, timing, and audience. Keep them in closed situations where they can express themselves in a controlled environment without antagonizing others.

Agitators are risk takers, but it is a result of their indomitable perspective. They can still be fearful of the unknown, so if you can give them reassurance regarding something they are working on, or even save them observation time by pointing out they are on the right track, you will earn some loyalty and potentially quash a revolt. They are not particularly formal, so this can be done in passing. The key is to keep them focused on the present, not on the past which they can complain about, or the future they tend to worry about. They are easily stressed out, and once they are, their ability to make wise decisions and behave according to social norms goes out the window.

PLACE ON YOUR TEAM

Agitators are unpredictable and easily bored. They are envious by nature, so often their comments are not just unhelpful to moving the organization forward, they're probably designed to disturb a situation based on personal traits or possessions rather than the greater organizational good. The Agitator does not belong on your team, and you should quickly move them out. To do so, make sure their immediate supervisor is documenting bad behavior, offering constructive discipline, and clearly outlining expected changes.

Until you are able to terminate the employment of the Agitator, deploy them where their natural pessimism and their eye to the worst-case scenario can be somewhat beneficial. Involve them in "what if" conversations where they can take the role of devil's advocate and keep them far from yourself and senior managers. As the old adage goes, *if you wrestle with skunks, you come out stinking.* Agitators can end up being accused of causing a hostile work environment, so make sure your managers know how to handle such situations and give yourself and senior management sufficient distance for plausible deniability. They are fairly imaginative, which is often what is behind their envy, so positions where they can visualize or fabricate will bring out their best.

Agitators are emotional. They can dish it out, but like most bullies, they cannot take it. They are not good team players because they force others to take the risks. They are quick to anger, so keep them away from group projects. And, if you have a suggestion box, consider getting rid of it until the Agitator is gone. They will use it to hurt the feelings of others and your job is to ensure that does not happen. If getting rid of a suggestion box is contrary to your company's goal of transparency and employee voice (good for you if it is), then have the reader of the suggestion box comments be someone with thick skin who knows what to share and with whom. Comments that are personal attacks should never be shared with the target, aka the victim.

It's difficult to find a reason to have Agitators on your team. When you want to remove them, you probably will need help from security.

THE SABOTEUR

"It's going to flood. I wonder how the dam broke."

PROFILE

The Saboteur is an Adversary, and the most dangerous of your employees. Saboteurs are narcissists who seek to make their mark on the world through fire-starting and a scorched-earth policy. They are egomaniacs who cannot tolerate any lack of adoration, so if they don't get their way, or if they find others viewing them as average or less than, the Saboteur will expeditiously send a missile to deflect, distract, or destroy. Their preference is to destroy because that simultaneously disarms, makes a point, and punishes.

Saboteurs are highly observant, and because doing damage is part of their DNA, they are especially good at identifying the weaknesses and vulnerabilities of others. This develops their keen sense of just where to direct a missile for the best strategic result and to cause the most damage.

The first thing that is noticeable about the Saboteur is how argumentative they are and how easily and quickly they make arguments personal. They seem always be angry and looking for an outlet or battle. If you have an employee who seems to be fighting with (not debating) several other employees, you have a Saboteur whose coworkers will tell HR that they would rather quit than have to work with them any longer. Often, sabotaging is a result of a need for attention or to harm a co-worker who's viewed as a competitor. The Saboteur rarely intends to hurt the organization, but they will resort to that if they think they are getting fired or disciplined, or if they view themselves as being treated unfairly. Not everyone will notice their disruptive and antagonistic behaviors at the same time. Proximity to the Saboteur matters. Those who work closely with them will feel the wrath first. Those who are at a distance may only see an interesting and captivating person who makes lofty promises. The Saboteur is conniving and will create short-term alliances for long-term goals. When it comes to the Saboteur, it is essential to compare notes across the organization and not take any one perspective. Eventually most people will see the danger in keeping the Saboteur on the payroll but, for many people, this will happen only after personal negative experiences.

Saboteurs are intolerant of the mistakes of others or the perceived inabilities of others. Instead of confrontations, they prefer to toy with people and push their buttons until the other person snaps or quits. Manipulating the emotions and actions of others is their primary goal at work. They are highly motivated by their ability to control other people and orchestrate situations. Because these efforts take up time, their workload will suffer unless they are also highly intelligent. They also are absent-minded and have trouble focusing, no doubt because they are paying too much attention to their plots to undermine others.

They are highly competitive and, therefore, arrogant or bitter since there will always be someone lesser and someone better. This causes them to be condescending and patronizing. Because of their insensitivity to others and their blatant attempts to bar the progress of their colleagues, Saboteurs are obvious outsiders. People will not be flocking to work on teams with them, carpool with them, or sit with them in the cafeteria. However, Saboteurs are not in a constant state of volatility. They can be productive until they cannot control their envy or a personal slight.

Sometimes their pessimism and negativity are not grounded in anything at work, making their behavior difficult to understand. But, regardless of the trigger, their behavior is the product of issues much deeper than what the organization can take on. They seek to create environments that are volatile and chaotic, and it should not matter to you if it is to get attention, harm someone, or satisfy a neurotic tendency.

TECHNIQUES TO MOTIVATE

Don't waste your time trying to fix this person or in finding the best seat on the bus for them. Their word cannot be trusted, and they will just tell you what you want to hear. Because their temper and instability are an extreme liability, this person needs to be identified and removed from your organization immediately. The Saboteur is not difficult to fire, as their destructive tendencies are usually quite obvious and their personnel file quite full. It is more difficult to notice them in your ranks when they are a brand new employee, working at a different location, or working among the rank and file who are less visible. Those who do notice might be fearful of rocking the ark. Some might not even have the sophistication to recognize what is happening, or they might not believe they have the authority to do anything about it. It will not be difficult to create a case against the Saboteur and prepare requisite paperwork for dismissal, but keep in mind that the risk in keeping them is greater than any risk in firing them prematurely or seemingly without cause. If you are in an at-will state, fire them now. If you are not, then get your paperwork in order, now.

PLACE ON YOUR TEAM

That's a no.